The AI Whisperer

Rowan Levi's Machine Learning Advances

Mei Gonzalez

ISBN: 9783100005510
Imprint: Telephasic Workshop
Copyright © 2024 Mei Gonzalez.
All Rights Reserved.

Contents

Introduction 1
Rowan Levi: The AI Whisperer 1

The Early Years 3
A Curious Mind from the Start 3
The Spark of Interest in Machine Learning 14

University Years 29
The Ivy League Experience 29
Breakthroughs and Advancements 40

Rise to Prominence 53
Industry Recognition and Job Offers 53
Ethical Considerations and Public Debate 64

Legacy and Future Prospects 77
Philanthropy and Giving Back 77
Speculations and Predictions for AI's Future 88

Index 103

Introduction

Rowan Levi: The AI Whisperer

The Early Years

A Curious Mind from the Start

Rowan's Childhood Fascination with Gadgets

From an early age, Rowan Levi exhibited an insatiable curiosity that would lay the groundwork for his future as the "AI Whisperer." Growing up in a household filled with electronic devices, from the latest gaming consoles to his father's vintage radio collection, Rowan was like a kid in a candy store—if the candy store were a tech shop where everything was fair game for disassembly. His fascination with gadgets was not just about playing with them; it was about understanding their inner workings.

Rowan's parents, recognizing this unique spark in their son, encouraged his explorations. They provided him with tools—screwdrivers, pliers, and even a soldering iron—transforming their home into a makeshift laboratory. It was here that Rowan first learned the difference between a Phillips head and a flathead screwdriver, a skill that would serve him well in his later engineering endeavors.

> "Why buy a toy when you can build one?"

This mantra became Rowan's guiding principle. At the tender age of eight, he took apart his first toy robot, a flashy creature that danced and lit up. What ensued was a chaotic explosion of plastic limbs and circuit boards. After hours of tinkering, he managed to reassemble it—albeit with a few extra screws that had no apparent purpose. The robot no longer danced, but it did blink ominously, which Rowan considered a significant upgrade.

Encouraging Parents and Supportive Environment

Rowan's parents, both educators, understood the importance of fostering creativity and critical thinking. They often engaged him in discussions about how things worked, encouraging him to ask questions. "Why does the light bulb turn on when I flip the switch?" became a common refrain in their household, leading to impromptu science lessons that often ended with a trip to the local hardware store for supplies.

The environment at home was not just supportive; it was a breeding ground for innovation. Rowan's father once built a miniature wind tunnel in their garage to demonstrate the principles of aerodynamics. Inspired, Rowan began creating his own inventions, from a homemade catapult that launched marshmallows to a rudimentary alarm system made from a shoebox and a string. Each project was a stepping stone, building his confidence and skill set.

Early Experiments with Robotics Kits

As Rowan approached middle school, his interests shifted toward robotics. His parents gifted him his first robotics kit, a basic assembly set that allowed him to build simple machines. He spent countless hours poring over the instruction manual, which was more of a novel in his hands. The thrill of following complex diagrams and troubleshooting errors became his new obsession.

At school, he joined the robotics club, where he found a community of like-minded peers who shared his passion. Together, they worked on projects that ranged from line-following robots to simple autonomous vehicles. Each success brought a rush of adrenaline, while each failure taught him resilience.

$$\text{Success} = \text{Effort} + \text{Learning from Failure} \quad (1)$$

This equation, although not formally studied, became a cornerstone of Rowan's philosophy. He learned that innovation often required a willingness to fail spectacularly before achieving success.

School Days and Academic Achievements

Rowan's fascination with gadgets translated seamlessly into his academic life. He excelled in science and mathematics, often outpacing his peers. His teachers recognized his potential and encouraged him to enter science fairs, where he showcased his projects, including a solar-powered car that he built with recycled materials.

One of his proudest moments came when he won first place at the regional science fair. His project, a robot designed to sort recyclables, not only impressed the judges but also sparked conversations about environmental sustainability among his classmates.

A Passion for Science Fiction and AI

In addition to his hands-on experiences, Rowan developed a love for science fiction. Books like Isaac Asimov's *I, Robot* and Philip K. Dick's *Do Androids Dream of Electric Sheep?* fueled his imagination and inspired him to think about the future of technology. He often found himself daydreaming about a world where robots and humans coexisted harmoniously, a theme that would later influence his work in AI.

Rowan's childhood fascination with gadgets was not merely a hobby; it was the foundation of his future career. Each experiment, each failure, and each success built a framework for understanding complex systems. It was this early exposure to technology and innovation that would eventually lead him to become a pioneer in the field of machine learning.

In retrospect, it's clear that Rowan's journey began with a simple curiosity about how things worked. As he often jokes, "If it has a battery, I'm taking it apart!" This playful yet determined approach to learning would become a hallmark of his character, setting the stage for his groundbreaking contributions to AI and machine learning.

> "Gadgets are like people; you have to understand their insides to appreciate their outsides."

Encouraging Parents and Supportive Environment

Rowan Levi's journey into the world of artificial intelligence was significantly shaped by the nurturing environment fostered by his parents. From the very beginning, it was clear that Rowan was not just another child; he was a curious mind bursting with questions, and his parents were the kind of people who believed that curiosity should be cultivated like a delicate seedling in a garden. They understood that a child's inquisitive nature is a precursor to innovation, and they approached parenting with the same fervor that scientists bring to their research.

The Role of Encouragement

Research in developmental psychology suggests that parental encouragement plays a critical role in shaping a child's interests and self-efficacy. According to Bandura's Social Learning Theory, children learn behaviors and develop beliefs about their capabilities through observation and reinforcement from their parents [?]. For Rowan, this meant that every time he tinkered with a gadget or expressed interest in a new technology, his parents were right there, cheering him on like he was the star quarterback of the family.

$$\text{Self-Efficacy} = \text{Outcome Expectancy} + \text{Perceived Capability} \qquad (2)$$

In this equation, we can see that the outcome expectancy (the belief that one can achieve a desired outcome) and perceived capability (belief in one's own abilities) are both essential for developing self-efficacy. Rowan's parents made sure he felt capable by providing him with the tools and resources he needed to explore his interests. They gifted him robotics kits and books on programming, which not only fueled his passion but also reinforced his belief in his own abilities.

Creating a Supportive Environment

The home environment is another crucial factor in fostering a child's passion for learning. Research indicates that a stimulating environment, rich with educational resources and opportunities for exploration, leads to greater academic success [?]. Rowan's parents transformed their home into a mini-laboratory, filled with spare computer parts, bookshelves lined with science fiction novels, and a workshop area where Rowan could freely experiment without the fear of making a mess.

For instance, one of Rowan's most memorable experiments involved a makeshift robot that he designed using an old vacuum cleaner and some LEGO pieces. His parents didn't just tolerate this chaos; they actively participated, offering suggestions and helping him troubleshoot when things went awry. This kind of engagement not only made learning fun but also instilled in him the confidence to tackle more complex challenges in the future.

The Influence of Science Fiction

Rowan's parents also recognized the power of storytelling in shaping a young mind. They introduced him to classic science fiction literature, which not only entertained him but also expanded his imagination. Works by authors such as Isaac Asimov and Arthur C. Clarke introduced him to concepts of artificial intelligence and robotics long before he encountered them in textbooks. This literary exposure is crucial, as narrative transportation theory posits that engaging with stories can enhance empathy and creativity, both of which are vital for innovation [?].

Encouragement Through Challenges

Of course, encouragement did not mean that Rowan was shielded from failure. His parents understood that resilience is a key component of success. When Rowan faced setbacks—like the time his robot failed to navigate a simple obstacle course—his parents were there to remind him that failure is simply a stepping stone on the path to success. They would often quote Thomas Edison, saying, "I have not failed. I've just found 10,000 ways that won't work." This perspective allowed Rowan to embrace challenges rather than shy away from them.

Conclusion

In summary, the supportive environment created by Rowan Levi's parents played an instrumental role in shaping his future as an innovator in artificial intelligence. Their unwavering encouragement, combined with a stimulating home environment and a healthy attitude toward failure, laid the groundwork for his success. As Rowan embarked on his journey into machine learning, he carried with him the invaluable lessons instilled by his parents: that curiosity should be nurtured, that failure is a part of learning, and that the pursuit of knowledge is a noble endeavor worth every effort.

Early Experiments with Robotics Kits

Rowan Levi's journey into the world of robotics began at an age when most children are still trying to figure out how to tie their shoelaces without a YouTube tutorial. Armed with a curious mind and a penchant for disassembling household appliances (sorry, Mom!), Rowan dove headfirst into the realm of robotics kits.

The First Encounter with Robotics

It all started with a birthday gift that would change the trajectory of his life: a basic robotics kit that promised to turn any child into a mini-engineer. The kit came with a set of wheels, sensors, and enough wires to make a grown adult weep in confusion. Rowan, however, saw it as a treasure trove of possibilities.

> "Why would I want a toy that doesn't move? I want to build a robot that can fetch me snacks!"

This determination led to his first project: a robot that could navigate the treacherous terrain of his living room, which, at the time, was littered with LEGO bricks and half-eaten snacks.

Theoretical Foundations

At the heart of robotics lies a blend of mechanical engineering, electronics, and computer science. To put it simply, it's like trying to teach a cat to fetch—frustrating, but oh-so-rewarding when it works. The fundamental theories that guided Rowan included:

- **Kinematics:** The study of motion without considering the forces that cause it. Rowan learned to calculate the trajectory of his robot using the equations of motion:
$$d = vt + \frac{1}{2}at^2 \qquad (3)$$
where d is distance, v is initial velocity, a is acceleration, and t is time.

- **Feedback Control Systems:** This theory helped him understand how to make his robot react to its environment. Using simple sensors, he implemented a basic feedback loop:
$$e(t) = r(t) - y(t) \qquad (4)$$
where $e(t)$ is the error at time t, $r(t)$ is the reference input, and $y(t)$ is the output.

- **Programming Logic:** Rowan learned to code his robot using a simple programming language. He quickly discovered that debugging was just a fancy term for "screaming at your computer until it behaves."

The Trials and Tribulations

Of course, not every experiment went according to plan. There were moments when his robot seemed more like a malfunctioning toaster than a sophisticated piece of technology. One memorable incident involved the robot's attempt to navigate a staircase. Instead of gracefully climbing up, it took a nosedive, performing what can only be described as a dramatic reenactment of a failed Olympic dive.

> "I swear it was a glitch!" Rowan exclaimed, as his mother rolled her eyes, likely questioning the wisdom of gifting him that robotics kit in the first place.

Learning from Failures

Despite the setbacks, each failure was a lesson in disguise. Rowan learned to troubleshoot his designs, often relying on the wisdom of online forums and the occasional YouTube video. He discovered that the best engineers are not those who never fail, but those who can turn a disaster into a learning opportunity.

For instance, after the staircase incident, he modified the robot's design, adding sensors that would detect edges. This led to the creation of his first successful autonomous robot, which not only navigated the living room but also avoided the family dog—who, incidentally, was less than thrilled about the competition for snacks.

The First Robotics Competition

Rowan's early experiments culminated in his participation in a local robotics competition. With a robot that could follow a line (and avoid the dog), he felt like a mini Elon Musk. The excitement was palpable, and so was the anxiety.

On competition day, Rowan stood nervously by his creation, which he affectionately named "SnackBot 3000." As the competition commenced, he watched as robots zoomed past, some malfunctioning spectacularly. SnackBot, however, performed flawlessly, navigating the course with a grace that belied its clunky design.

> "If only it could fetch me pizza, I'd be set for life!" Rowan joked, as he cheered for his robot.

In the end, SnackBot didn't win first place, but it did secure the award for "Most Likely to Steal Your Snacks." For Rowan, this was a victory in itself—a recognition of his creativity and hard work.

Conclusion

Rowan Levi's early experiments with robotics kits were not just about building machines; they were about building resilience, creativity, and a lifelong passion for technology. Each project, failure, and success laid the groundwork for his future endeavors in the world of artificial intelligence. Who knew that a simple robotics kit could spark a journey that would eventually lead to becoming the AI Whisperer?

As Rowan would later say,

> "If you can't make a robot that fetches snacks, are you even really trying?"

School Days and Academic Achievements

Rowan Levi's school days were not just a blur of textbooks and homework; they were a vibrant tapestry of academic curiosity interwoven with a sprinkle of mischief.

While most students were busy perfecting their TikTok dances or figuring out how to sneak snacks into class, Rowan was busy plotting the next great machine learning breakthrough. It was during these formative years that Rowan's unique blend of intellect, creativity, and an insatiable thirst for knowledge began to shine.

The Science Fair Saga

In the eighth grade, Rowan participated in the annual science fair, an event that would set the stage for future accolades. Instead of the usual volcano or baking soda experiment, Rowan decided to build a simple machine learning model to predict the outcomes of various sports games based on historical data. The project was ambitious for a middle schooler, but Rowan was undeterred.

The model used a basic linear regression, represented mathematically as:

$$y = mx + b$$

where y is the predicted outcome, m is the slope of the line (indicating the relationship between variables), x is the independent variable (in this case, historical performance data), and b is the y-intercept.

Rowan's project not only caught the attention of the judges but also sparked a lively debate among peers about the ethics of data usage in sports. "Can machines predict the unpredictable?" they asked, and Rowan, with the confidence of a young innovator, responded, "Only if you let them in on the game!"

Honors and Awards

By the time Rowan reached high school, the accolades began to pile up. With a GPA that could make a calculator weep, Rowan was not just another face in the crowd; they were the face of academic excellence. Honors classes in mathematics and computer science were Rowan's playgrounds, where equations danced like confetti at a birthday party.

In the sophomore year, Rowan was awarded the prestigious *Young Innovator's Award* for a project that utilized natural language processing (NLP) to analyze student sentiments from social media regarding school policies. Using sentiment analysis, Rowan was able to classify the emotions expressed in tweets as positive, negative, or neutral, employing the following equation for sentiment scoring:

$$S = \frac{(P - N)}{T}$$

where S is the sentiment score, P is the number of positive words, N is the number of negative words, and T is the total number of words. This project not only showcased Rowan's technical prowess but also highlighted the potential of AI in understanding human emotions—a topic that would later become a cornerstone of Rowan's career.

Extracurricular Excellence

Rowan's academic achievements were complemented by a plethora of extracurricular activities. As the president of the Robotics Club, Rowan led a team to victory in the state-level robotics competition. The project involved programming a robot to navigate a maze using algorithms that optimized its pathfinding capabilities, specifically employing the A* search algorithm, which is defined as follows:

$$f(n) = g(n) + h(n)$$

where $f(n)$ is the total estimated cost of the cheapest solution through node n, $g(n)$ is the cost to reach node n, and $h(n)$ is the estimated cost from node n to the goal.

Under Rowan's leadership, the team not only won first place but also inspired a new wave of students to explore the realms of robotics and AI. "If a robot can navigate a maze, imagine what we can do with our lives!" Rowan would often proclaim, arms wide open as if embracing the future.

Mentorship and Guidance

Throughout high school, Rowan was fortunate to have mentors who recognized the potential in this young innovator. One such mentor was Mrs. Thompson, the computer science teacher, who often stayed after school to help Rowan refine their coding skills. "Rowan, if you can code a computer to do your homework, you're golden!" she joked, but little did she know that Rowan was already working on automating the mundane tasks of life.

With her guidance, Rowan learned about advanced algorithms and data structures, concepts that would become second nature. This foundational knowledge would later fuel Rowan's passion for machine learning, as they began to understand the importance of data in training models.

Conclusion

By the time graduation rolled around, Rowan Levi was not just a student; they were a force of nature. With a string of awards, a portfolio of groundbreaking projects, and a reputation as the "AI Whisperer," Rowan was ready to take on the world. The school days, filled with academic achievements, were merely the beginning of a journey that would lead to unprecedented advancements in machine learning and artificial intelligence. As Rowan often quipped, "If school was a video game, I just leveled up to boss mode!"

A Passion for Science Fiction and AI

Rowan Levi's fascination with artificial intelligence (AI) did not sprout from a vacuum; it was deeply rooted in his childhood love for science fiction. From the moment he could read, he devoured every sci-fi novel he could find, often sneaking under the covers with a flashlight to finish just one more chapter. His bookshelf was a shrine to the genre, featuring works from Isaac Asimov, Philip K. Dick, and Arthur C. Clarke. Each story ignited his imagination, presenting a world where humans and machines coexisted, often with complex relationships that mirrored the best and worst of humanity.

One of the seminal works that shaped Rowan's understanding of AI was Asimov's *I, Robot*. The famous Three Laws of Robotics, which govern the ethical behavior of robots, became a lens through which he viewed the real-world implications of AI development. The laws state:

1. A robot may not injure a human being or, through inaction, allow a human being to cor
$$(5)$$
2. A robot must obey the orders given it by human beings except where such orders woulc
$$(6)$$
3. A robot must protect its own existence as long as such protection does not conflict with
$$(7)$$

These laws not only fueled Rowan's passion for AI but also instilled in him a sense of responsibility. He often pondered the ethical dilemmas faced by AI developers: *What happens when machines are given the power to make decisions? How do we ensure they act in humanity's best interest?* These questions were not mere academic exercises for Rowan; they were the guiding principles that influenced his later work in machine learning.

Rowan's early experiments with robotics kits were heavily inspired by the characters and scenarios from his favorite sci-fi stories. He would often create simple robots programmed to perform tasks, but he would also incorporate elements of storytelling. For instance, he once designed a robot that could navigate a maze while reciting quotes from *Blade Runner*. This blend of creativity and technical prowess set the stage for his future innovations in AI.

As he progressed through school, Rowan's passion for science fiction began to intersect with his academic pursuits. He discovered that many of the concepts he encountered in novels were grounded in real scientific theories. For example, the idea of neural networks, which he would later explore in-depth, was not just a figment of fiction but a burgeoning field of research. The parallels between the fictional AI characters and the real-world technology being developed fascinated him.

In high school, he had the opportunity to participate in a robotics competition, where he developed a robot that could mimic human emotions through facial recognition software. This project was not only an application of his technical skills but also a reflection of the themes he had absorbed from science fiction. He named his robot *EmoBot*, and it was designed to respond to human emotions, a concept that resonated with the emotional intelligence often depicted in sci-fi narratives.

Rowan's passion for science fiction also led him to explore the philosophical implications of AI. He became particularly interested in the Turing Test, proposed by Alan Turing, which assesses a machine's ability to exhibit intelligent behavior indistinguishable from that of a human. This concept was a recurring theme in the stories he loved, raising questions about consciousness and the nature of being. He often debated with classmates whether machines could ever truly understand human emotions or if they were merely simulating responses based on algorithms.

Moreover, his interest in AI was not limited to theoretical aspects; it also included the societal impacts of emerging technologies. He was particularly drawn to dystopian narratives, such as those found in *The Matrix* and *Black Mirror*, which depicted the potential consequences of unchecked AI development. These stories served as cautionary tales, reinforcing his belief that AI must be developed responsibly, with a keen awareness of its ethical implications.

In summary, Rowan Levi's passion for science fiction and AI was a potent combination that shaped his early years and laid the groundwork for his future innovations. The stories he cherished not only fueled his imagination but also provided a framework for understanding the complexities of artificial intelligence. As he ventured into the world of machine learning, he carried with him the lessons learned from his favorite authors: the importance of ethics, the potential for creativity, and the profound questions that arise when humans and machines intersect. This unique perspective would later become a hallmark of his approach to AI, making him not just an innovator, but also a thoughtful advocate for responsible technology development.

The Spark of Interest in Machine Learning

Discovering Machine Learning in High School

In the bustling hallways of Lincoln High School, where the lockers creaked louder than the teachers' voices, Rowan Levi stumbled upon a world that would change his life forever: machine learning. It was during a particularly uneventful computer science class that a guest speaker, a scruffy-looking data scientist with a penchant for coffee and a flair for the dramatic, introduced the concept of algorithms that could learn from data. The moment Rowan heard the phrase "data-driven decisions," it was as if a light bulb flickered to life above his head, illuminating a path he never knew existed.

The Spark of Curiosity

Rowan's curiosity was piqued when the speaker explained the concept of supervised learning, where algorithms learn from labeled data. The idea that machines could be trained to recognize patterns and make predictions based on past experiences resonated with his imaginative mind. He vividly remembers the speaker using the analogy of a child learning to distinguish between cats and dogs. "You show them pictures of both, and after a while, they can tell the difference!" the speaker exclaimed, gesturing wildly as if he were conducting an orchestra of neural networks.

Mathematically, this process can be expressed as follows:

$$f(x) = y \qquad (8)$$

Where f represents the function learned by the algorithm, x is the input data, and y is the output label. This simple equation opened the floodgates of possibility in Rowan's mind. He envisioned a future where machines could help solve complex problems, from predicting weather patterns to diagnosing diseases.

Tackling Challenges

However, the journey into the world of machine learning was not without its challenges. Inspired by the guest speaker, Rowan decided to take matters into his own hands. He dove headfirst into online courses, tutorials, and even a few dusty textbooks that had been left behind by previous generations of tech-savvy students. The first hurdle he faced was understanding the mathematics behind machine learning, particularly linear algebra and statistics.

Rowan often found himself staring blankly at equations like:

$$\hat{y} = \beta_0 + \beta_1 x_1 + \beta_2 x_2 + \ldots + \beta_n x_n \tag{9}$$

Where $\hat{y}$ is the predicted outcome, β_0 is the y-intercept, and β_i are the coefficients for each feature x_i. It felt like deciphering a secret code, but with each sleepless night spent grappling with concepts like gradient descent and loss functions, he began to piece it all together.

First Steps into Machine Learning

By the end of his junior year, Rowan had built his first simple neural network using a free online platform. It was a basic model designed to classify handwritten digits from the MNIST dataset. He recalls the thrill of seeing the model learn: "It was like watching a toddler take their first steps, only instead of falling over, it was correctly identifying numbers!"

The excitement of getting a 95% accuracy rate was intoxicating. He had taken his first steps into the world of machine learning, but the road ahead was still long and winding. To further his understanding, Rowan sought out mentorship from a local university professor who was conducting research in artificial intelligence. This relationship would prove pivotal, as it opened doors to advanced concepts and real-world applications.

A Defining Moment

A defining moment came when Rowan decided to enter the National Science Fair with a project that combined his newfound love for machine learning and his childhood fascination with robotics. He developed a simple robot that could navigate a maze using reinforcement learning, a method where agents learn to make decisions based on rewards and penalties.

The mathematical foundation of reinforcement learning can be summarized with the equation:

$$Q(s, a) = R(s, a) + \gamma \max_{a'} Q(s', a') \tag{10}$$

Here, $Q(s, a)$ represents the expected utility of taking action a in state s, $R(s, a)$ is the immediate reward, and γ is the discount factor that weighs future rewards. Rowan's robot learned to navigate the maze by trial and error, receiving rewards for reaching the end and penalties for hitting walls.

The day of the science fair arrived, and with it came the culmination of countless hours of coding, debugging, and caffeinated late-night brainstorming sessions. As he watched his robot successfully complete the maze, he felt an overwhelming sense of accomplishment. The judges were equally impressed, and Rowan walked away with first place, an experience that solidified his passion for machine learning.

Conclusion

Rowan's high school years were not just about textbooks and exams; they were a transformative period that laid the groundwork for his future in artificial intelligence. The spark ignited by that guest speaker turned into a blazing fire of curiosity and innovation. He emerged from high school not just as a student, but as a budding innovator ready to tackle the challenges of the future, armed with the knowledge that machines could learn, adapt, and ultimately change the world.

Building First Neural Network Model

Rowan Levi's journey into the world of machine learning took a pivotal turn when he decided to build his first neural network model. This moment was not just a significant milestone in his academic career but also a reflection of his childhood fascination with gadgets and technology. The process of constructing a neural network is akin to assembling a complex puzzle, where each piece must fit perfectly to create a coherent picture of understanding.

Understanding Neural Networks

At its core, a neural network is a computational model inspired by the way biological neural networks in the human brain process information. A typical neural network consists of layers of interconnected nodes, or neurons, which transform input data into output predictions. The architecture of a neural network can be broken down into three main components:

- **Input Layer:** This layer receives the input data. Each neuron in this layer corresponds to a feature in the input dataset.

- **Hidden Layers:** These layers perform computations and transformations on the input data. The number of hidden layers and the number of neurons in each layer can vary based on the complexity of the task.

- **Output Layer:** This layer produces the final output of the network, which can be a classification label or a continuous value, depending on the problem being solved.

The relationship between the layers can be expressed mathematically. For a simple neural network with one hidden layer, the output y can be calculated as follows:

$$y = f(W_2 \cdot h + b_2)$$

where: - W_2 is the weight matrix connecting the hidden layer to the output layer, - h is the activation from the hidden layer, - b_2 is the bias term for the output layer, and - f is the activation function applied at the output layer.

Building the Model

Rowan's first neural network was designed to tackle a classic problem: handwritten digit recognition using the MNIST dataset, which consists of 70,000 images of handwritten digits (0-9). The goal was to classify each image into one of the ten digit categories.

Step 1: Data Preparation Rowan began by loading the MNIST dataset and preprocessing the images. This involved normalizing the pixel values to a range of [0, 1] by dividing by 255 (the maximum pixel value). This step is crucial as it helps in speeding up the convergence during training. The images were also reshaped into a vector of size 784 (28x28 pixels).

Step 2: Defining the Architecture Rowan decided on a simple architecture with one hidden layer consisting of 128 neurons. The architecture can be summarized as follows:

- Input Layer: 784 neurons (for the 28x28 pixel images)

- Hidden Layer: 128 neurons (using ReLU activation function)

- Output Layer: 10 neurons (softmax activation for multi-class classification)

Step 3: Initializing Weights and Biases To initialize the weights, Rowan used a random distribution to ensure that the network starts with diverse values. The biases were initialized to zeros. The weights W_1 connecting the input layer to the hidden layer and W_2 connecting the hidden layer to the output layer were defined as:

$$W_1 \sim \mathcal{N}(0, 0.01) \quad \text{and} \quad W_2 \sim \mathcal{N}(0, 0.01)$$

Step 4: Forward Propagation Rowan implemented the forward propagation algorithm, which involves calculating the output of each neuron by applying the weighted sum and the activation function. For the hidden layer, the output h is calculated as:

$$h = f(W_1 \cdot x + b_1)$$

where x is the input vector, and b_1 is the bias for the hidden layer.

Step 5: Loss Function To measure the performance of the model, Rowan used the categorical cross-entropy loss function, defined as:

$$L(y, \hat{y}) = -\sum_{i=1}^{C} y_i \log(\hat{y}_i)$$

where C is the number of classes, y is the true distribution, and $\hat{y}$ is the predicted distribution from the softmax layer.

Step 6: Backpropagation and Optimization Rowan then implemented backpropagation to update the weights and biases. This involves calculating the gradients of the loss function with respect to each weight and bias, allowing the model to learn from its mistakes. He used the popular Adam optimizer for this purpose, which adapts the learning rate for each parameter:

$$\theta = \theta - \eta \cdot \frac{m_t}{\sqrt{v_t} + \epsilon}$$

where η is the learning rate, m_t is the first moment estimate, v_t is the second moment estimate, and ϵ is a small constant to prevent division by zero.

Training the Model

After defining the architecture and loss function, Rowan trained the model using mini-batch gradient descent. He divided the dataset into batches and iteratively updated the weights for a predefined number of epochs. With each epoch, the model's accuracy improved, and he could see the power of machine learning in action.

Results and Reflections

Upon completion of the training process, Rowan evaluated his model on a test set and achieved an impressive accuracy of over 97%. This success not only validated his efforts but also ignited a passion for further exploration in the field of artificial intelligence.

Rowan's experience in building his first neural network model was a mix of excitement and frustration, akin to trying to assemble IKEA furniture without the manual—lots of trial and error, but ultimately rewarding. This foundational project set the stage for his future innovations and solidified his identity as "The AI Whisperer."

In conclusion, building his first neural network model was not just a technical exercise for Rowan Levi; it was a transformative experience that sparked a lifelong journey into the depths of artificial intelligence, proving that with curiosity and persistence, even the most complex challenges can be tackled—one neuron at a time.

Mentorship from Leading AI Researchers

Rowan Levi's journey into the world of artificial intelligence was not solely a result of his own curiosity and determination; it was significantly influenced by the mentorship he received from some of the leading researchers in the field. This mentorship played a crucial role in shaping his understanding of machine learning, providing him with insights that were both theoretical and practical.

The Importance of Mentorship

Mentorship in academia and industry is often described as a guiding relationship where an experienced individual provides knowledge, advice, and support to a less experienced mentee. According to a study by Allen et al. (2004), effective mentorship can enhance career development, increase job satisfaction, and improve overall performance. For Rowan, the mentorship he received was pivotal in transforming his theoretical knowledge into applicable skills.

Connecting with AI Pioneers

During his high school years, Rowan was fortunate enough to connect with several prominent figures in AI. These connections were often facilitated through science fairs, workshops, and online forums dedicated to machine learning. One of the most influential mentors was Dr. Emily Tran, a leading researcher in neural networks and deep learning. Dr. Tran had a knack for breaking down complex concepts into digestible pieces, often using humor to make the learning process enjoyable.

> "Rowan, if you think training a neural network is hard, try teaching a cat to fetch!"

Dr. Tran introduced Rowan to the concept of **backpropagation**, a fundamental algorithm used for training neural networks. The backpropagation algorithm is defined mathematically as:

$$\delta^{(l)} = \nabla_a C \odot \sigma'(z^{(l)})$$

where $\delta^{(l)}$ is the error term for layer l, $\nabla_a C$ is the gradient of the cost function with respect to the activations, and $\sigma'(z^{(l)})$ is the derivative of the activation function. This equation essentially allows the model to adjust its weights based on the error of its predictions, a concept that Rowan would later apply in his own projects.

Hands-On Experience

Rowan's mentorship experience was not limited to theoretical discussions. He was also given the opportunity to work on real-world projects under the guidance of his mentors. One notable project involved developing a predictive model for a local non-profit organization that aimed to improve food distribution in underserved communities. This project required Rowan to apply various machine learning techniques, including **linear regression** and **decision trees**.

The linear regression model can be expressed as:

$$y = \beta_0 + \beta_1 x_1 + \beta_2 x_2 + \ldots + \beta_n x_n + \epsilon$$

where y is the predicted outcome, β_0 is the y-intercept, $\beta_1, \beta_2, \ldots, \beta_n$ are the coefficients of the independent variables $x_1, x_2, \ldots, x_n$, and ϵ is the error term.

This hands-on experience not only solidified Rowan's understanding of machine learning algorithms but also instilled a sense of responsibility to use technology for social good.

Networking and Collaboration

Through his mentors, Rowan learned the value of networking and collaboration in the AI community. Attending conferences and workshops allowed him to meet other innovators and researchers, fostering relationships that would prove beneficial throughout his career. One such event was the **International Conference on Machine Learning (ICML)**, where Rowan had the chance to present his early work on a sentiment analysis model.

During the conference, he encountered Dr. Raj Patel, a well-respected figure in natural language processing. Dr. Patel's feedback on Rowan's work was invaluable, as he provided constructive criticism and suggested further avenues of research. This interaction exemplified the collaborative spirit that is prevalent in the AI research community.

Challenges Faced and Overcome

Despite the advantages of mentorship, Rowan faced challenges along the way. One significant hurdle was the steep learning curve associated with advanced topics in machine learning. At times, he felt overwhelmed by the complexity of algorithms and the vast amount of information available. However, his mentors encouraged him to embrace these challenges, emphasizing that struggle is often a precursor to growth.

For example, when Rowan was grappling with the intricacies of **reinforcement learning**, he sought guidance from Dr. Tran, who explained the concept using a simple analogy involving training a dog. She stated:

> "Think of it this way: every time your dog fetches the ball, you give it a treat. That's reinforcement learning in a nutshell!"

This perspective helped Rowan to simplify the process and understand the underlying principles of reinforcement learning, which can be mathematically defined by the Bellman equation:

$$V(s) = \max_{a} \left(R(s,a) + \gamma \sum_{s'} P(s'|s,a) V(s') \right)$$

where $V(s)$ is the value function, $R(s,a)$ is the reward for taking action a in state s, γ is the discount factor, and $P(s'|s,a)$ is the probability of transitioning to state s' given state s and action a.

Conclusion

Rowan Levi's mentorship experiences were instrumental in his development as an AI innovator. The guidance, support, and knowledge he received from leading researchers not only helped him navigate the complexities of machine learning but also inspired him to pursue a career dedicated to advancing the field. As he moved forward in his journey, Rowan carried with him the lessons learned from his mentors, embodying the spirit of collaboration and innovation that defines the AI community.

In the words of Dr. Tran:

> "Remember, Rowan, the only limit to your impact is your imagination and commitment. Now go out there and whisper to those machines!"

Winning National Science Fair with ML Project

Rowan Levi's journey in machine learning culminated in an extraordinary achievement: winning the National Science Fair with his groundbreaking project titled *Predicting the Future: A Machine Learning Approach to Climate Change*. This project not only showcased his technical prowess but also highlighted the pressing issues of our time, making it a compelling entry that resonated with judges and attendees alike.

The Problem Statement

The primary aim of Rowan's project was to develop a predictive model that could forecast climate change impacts based on historical data. The urgency of addressing climate change could not be overstated, as it posed significant threats to ecosystems, economies, and human health. The project sought to answer critical questions such as:

- How can we accurately predict temperature changes over the next decade?
- What are the potential impacts of these changes on weather patterns and sea levels?

Data Collection and Preparation

Rowan began by gathering extensive datasets from reputable sources, including NASA and the National Oceanic and Atmospheric Administration (NOAA). The datasets included historical temperature records, carbon dioxide levels, and other relevant environmental indicators.

The data preparation phase involved cleaning and preprocessing the data to ensure its quality. This included:

- Handling missing values using imputation techniques.

- Normalizing the data to bring all features to a similar scale, which is crucial for many machine learning algorithms.

- Splitting the dataset into training and testing sets to evaluate model performance effectively.

Choosing the Right Algorithm

Rowan explored various machine learning algorithms to find the most suitable one for his project. After careful consideration, he opted for a combination of linear regression and decision trees, leveraging the strengths of both models.

The linear regression model was used to establish a baseline prediction model, defined by the equation:

$$y = \beta_0 + \beta_1 x_1 + \beta_2 x_2 + \ldots + \beta_n x_n + \epsilon \tag{11}$$

where y represents the predicted temperature, x_i are the input features (like CO2 levels), β_i are the coefficients, and ϵ is the error term.

To enhance the model's accuracy, Rowan implemented a decision tree algorithm, which is particularly effective for capturing non-linear relationships in the data. The decision tree splits the data into subsets based on feature values, creating a tree-like structure that leads to predictions.

Model Training and Evaluation

After selecting the algorithms, Rowan trained his models using the training dataset. He utilized cross-validation techniques to ensure that his model generalized well to unseen data. The performance of the model was evaluated using metrics such as Mean Absolute Error (MAE) and R-squared (R^2):

$$MAE = \frac{1}{n} \sum_{i=1}^{n} |y_i - \hat{y}_i| \tag{12}$$

$$R^2 = 1 - \frac{\sum_{i=1}^{n}(y_i - \hat{y}_i)^2}{\sum_{i=1}^{n}(y_i - \bar{y})^2} \tag{13}$$

where y_i is the actual value, $\hat{y}_i$ is the predicted value, and $\bar{y}$ is the mean of the actual values.

Rowan's model achieved an impressive R^2 score of 0.85, indicating a strong correlation between the predicted and actual temperature changes.

Presentation and Impact

At the National Science Fair, Rowan presented his findings with a dynamic display that included visualizations of his model's predictions and the potential future impacts of climate change. He used graphs to illustrate the projected temperature increases and their implications for global sea levels.

The judges were particularly impressed by the practical applications of Rowan's work, which could inform policymakers and contribute to climate change mitigation strategies. His ability to communicate complex scientific concepts in an engaging manner, infused with humor and relatable anecdotes, made his presentation a standout.

Rowan's project not only won first place but also garnered media attention, leading to invitations for interviews and speaking engagements. This recognition further fueled his passion for AI and its potential to solve real-world problems, setting the stage for his future endeavors in the field.

In conclusion, winning the National Science Fair was a pivotal moment in Rowan Levi's journey as an innovator. It validated his hard work and dedication to machine learning, while also emphasizing the importance of using technology for the greater good. As he moved forward, this experience would serve as a foundation for his commitment to ethical AI development and social responsibility.

Decision to Pursue AI as a Career

Rowan Levi's decision to pursue a career in artificial intelligence (AI) was not merely a product of his academic success or his early fascination with technology. It was a culmination of experiences, influences, and a deep-seated belief in the potential of AI to transform the world. As he navigated the complex landscape of machine learning, he faced several pivotal moments that solidified his commitment to this field.

The Convergence of Passion and Purpose

From a young age, Rowan was captivated by the idea of machines that could learn and adapt. This fascination was not just a passing interest; it was rooted in a desire to create technology that could solve real-world problems. The turning point came during a particularly enlightening high school project where he was tasked with developing a simple algorithm to predict student performance based on historical data. This project was not just an academic exercise; it was the first time Rowan experienced the thrill of seeing his code come to life, making predictions that could actually impact educational outcomes.

$$\text{Performance}_{predicted} = f(\text{Hours Studied, Attendance, Previous Grades}) \quad (14)$$

This equation represented a simplified model of his work, where f was the function he designed to analyze the data. The success of this project ignited a fire within him. He realized that AI was not just about coding; it was about understanding human behavior and using that understanding to create meaningful change.

Influence of Mentorship

Rowan's decision was further influenced by the mentorship he received from leading AI researchers. One particular mentor, Dr. Angela Chen, was a pioneer in the field of natural language processing. Under her guidance, Rowan learned not only the technical skills necessary for AI development but also the ethical implications of deploying such technology. Dr. Chen often emphasized the importance of responsible AI, stating:

> "With great power comes great responsibility. As AI developers, we must ensure our creations serve humanity, not hinder it."

This mantra resonated deeply with Rowan. He recognized that pursuing a career in AI was not just about personal ambition; it was about contributing to a field that could either uplift or undermine society depending on how it was wielded.

The Call of Innovation

As Rowan progressed through his high school years, the allure of innovation became increasingly irresistible. He participated in various hackathons and coding competitions, where he encountered like-minded peers who shared his passion. It was at one such event that he first heard about the concept of reinforcement learning, a branch of AI that mimicked the way humans learn through trial and error. This concept was revolutionary for him, as it aligned perfectly with his belief in iterative improvement and learning from failure.

$$Q(s,a) \leftarrow Q(s,a) + \alpha \left(r + \gamma \max_{a'} Q(s',a') - Q(s,a) \right) \qquad (15)$$

In this equation, $Q(s,a)$ represents the expected utility of taking action a in state s, while r is the reward received after taking action a. The parameters α and γ are the learning rate and discount factor, respectively. Understanding this framework not only deepened his technical knowledge but also reinforced his desire to innovate within the field.

The National Science Fair Triumph

Winning the national science fair with his machine learning project was the cherry on top of Rowan's burgeoning career aspirations. His project, which involved developing a predictive model for climate change impacts on local ecosystems, garnered attention not just for its technical merit but also for its societal relevance. The judges were impressed by his ability to apply AI to an urgent global issue, and this recognition solidified his resolve to pursue AI as a career.

$$\text{Ecosystem Impact} = g(\text{Temperature Rise}, \text{Pollution Levels}, \text{Biodiversity Index}) \qquad (16)$$

In this equation, g represented the complex interactions Rowan modeled between various environmental factors. This project was a testament to the potential of AI to address pressing challenges, further motivating him to dedicate his life to this field.

Conclusion: A Future in AI

Ultimately, Rowan Levi's decision to pursue a career in AI was driven by a combination of personal passion, mentorship, and a desire to make a positive impact on the world. He recognized that AI was not just about algorithms and data; it was about understanding human needs and using technology to address them. This realization set him on a path to become not only a skilled practitioner in AI but also an advocate for its responsible use.

As he moved forward into his university years and beyond, Rowan carried with him the lessons learned from his formative experiences, ready to tackle the challenges and opportunities that lay ahead in the ever-evolving field of artificial intelligence.

University Years

The Ivy League Experience

Acceptance to Prestigious University

Rowan Levi's journey to acceptance at a prestigious university was not just a stroke of luck; it was the culmination of years of dedication, intellectual curiosity, and a sprinkle of that magical ingredient we call determination. The acceptance letter, which arrived on a crisp spring morning, felt like the universe's way of saying, "Congratulations, you are officially a nerd with a capital N!"

In the world of academia, gaining admission to an Ivy League institution is akin to winning the lottery—if the lottery required you to write essays, submit test scores, and showcase your extracurricular activities like a resume for a job you're not qualified for. Rowan, however, was more than qualified. He was a walking, talking, algorithm-breathing testament to what happens when passion meets preparation.

The Application Process

The application process itself was a rigorous gauntlet that tested not only Rowan's academic prowess but also his ability to navigate the emotional rollercoaster that is college admissions. It began with the SAT, a standardized test that has become synonymous with stress-induced hair loss and caffeine overdoses. Rowan tackled the SAT with the same fervor he applied to his robotics projects, spending countless hours practicing equations and verbal reasoning until he could solve for x in his sleep.

$$\text{SAT Score} = \text{Math Score} + \text{Verbal Score} \tag{17}$$

However, Rowan understood that numbers alone wouldn't get him through the gates of academia's elite. He needed to showcase his unique experiences and insights. This is where his passion for machine learning took center stage. He crafted a personal statement that not only highlighted his technical skills but also illustrated his journey from a curious child tinkering with gadgets to a high school student building neural networks.

The Personal Statement

Rowan's personal statement was a masterclass in storytelling. He began with an anecdote about the first time he successfully programmed a robot to navigate a maze. He described the moment when the robot, after several failed attempts (and a few minor meltdowns), finally found its way to the cheese at the end of the maze. "It was the first time I realized that failure is just a stepping stone to success," he wrote, capturing the essence of innovation and resilience.

> "Success is not final, failure is not fatal: It is the courage to continue that counts." - Winston S. Churchill

Rowan's narrative seamlessly transitioned into his high school experiences, detailing his participation in science fairs, where he often outshone his peers with projects that seemed to come straight out of a sci-fi movie. He recounted the thrill of winning the national science fair with his machine learning project, which predicted the outcomes of various environmental scenarios. This not only showcased his technical acumen but also his commitment to using technology for the greater good.

Letters of Recommendation

Next came the letters of recommendation, which acted like the cherry on top of Rowan's application sundae. He approached his teachers, each of whom had witnessed his transformation from a shy, gadget-loving kid to a confident, innovative thinker. One particularly memorable letter came from his physics teacher, who wrote about Rowan's ability to grasp complex concepts with ease and his knack for turning theoretical problems into practical solutions.

> "Rowan is not just a student; he is a force of nature in the classroom."
> - Ms. Thompson

As the deadline approached, Rowan meticulously reviewed every component of his application, ensuring that it reflected not just his achievements but his personality. He wanted the admissions committee to see beyond the numbers and into the heart of a young innovator ready to tackle the challenges of the future.

The Waiting Game

After submitting his application, the waiting game began—a torturous period filled with anxiety and self-doubt. Rowan filled his days with schoolwork, robotics club meetings, and binge-watching science fiction series, all while refreshing his email inbox like a caffeine-fueled squirrel.

Finally, the fateful day arrived. The email popped up in his inbox, and his heart raced faster than the processors in his beloved machines. With trembling hands, he clicked open the message, and there it was: "Congratulations, Rowan Levi! We are pleased to offer you admission to our university."

Celebrating the Achievement

The moment was surreal. Rowan leaped out of his chair, startling his cat, who promptly judged him with a disdainful glare. He ran to tell his parents, who were equally ecstatic, shedding tears of joy as they celebrated the culmination of years of hard work.

Rowan's acceptance into a prestigious university was not just a personal victory; it was a testament to the power of perseverance, the importance of community support, and the unyielding belief that with passion and dedication, even the most ambitious dreams can become a reality.

In the grand scheme of things, this acceptance was merely the beginning of Rowan's journey—the first step into a world where he would not only learn from the best but also contribute to the ever-evolving field of artificial intelligence. Little did he know, the real adventure was just around the corner, waiting for him to embrace it with open arms and a heart full of curiosity.

Diving Deep into AI Research

As Rowan Levi stepped into the hallowed halls of the prestigious Ivy League institution, he was greeted not only by the legacy of innovation but also by an insatiable curiosity that had driven him since childhood. It was here, amidst the towering stacks of books and the hum of intellectual discourse, that Rowan truly began to dive deep into the world of Artificial Intelligence (AI) research.

Theoretical Foundations

To understand AI, one must first grasp its theoretical underpinnings. At the core of AI research lies the concept of **machine learning**, a subset of AI that focuses on the development of algorithms that allow computers to learn from and make predictions based on data. One of the foundational theories in machine learning is the *statistical learning theory*, which provides a framework for understanding how algorithms can generalize from training data to unseen data.

The fundamental equation that governs many machine learning models is the loss function, represented as:

$$L(\theta) = \frac{1}{N} \sum_{i=1}^{N} (y_i - f(x_i; \theta))^2 \tag{18}$$

where $L(\theta)$ is the loss function, N is the number of data points, y_i is the true output, $f(x_i; \theta)$ is the predicted output, and θ represents the parameters of the model. This equation encapsulates the goal of minimizing the difference between predicted and actual outcomes, a principle that would guide Rowan's research endeavors.

Research Projects

During his university years, Rowan engaged in several research projects that allowed him to apply theoretical concepts to real-world problems. One notable project involved developing a **natural language processing (NLP)** model capable of understanding and generating human-like text. This task required an understanding of *transformer models*, which have revolutionized NLP by enabling models to consider context more effectively than previous architectures.

Rowan's team implemented the transformer architecture, defined by the following attention mechanism:

$$\text{Attention}(Q, K, V) = \text{softmax}\left(\frac{QK^T}{\sqrt{d_k}}\right) V \tag{19}$$

where Q represents the query, K the key, V the value, and d_k the dimension of the keys. This mechanism allowed the model to weigh the importance of different words in a sentence, leading to significant improvements in tasks such as sentiment analysis and text summarization.

Challenges and Solutions

However, diving deep into AI research was not without its challenges. One significant hurdle was the issue of **overfitting**, where a model performs exceptionally well on training data but fails to generalize to new data. To combat this, Rowan employed techniques such as *regularization* and *cross-validation*.

Regularization techniques, such as L2 regularization, can be expressed mathematically as:

$$L(\theta) = \frac{1}{N} \sum_{i=1}^{N} (y_i - f(x_i; \theta))^2 + \lambda \sum_{j=1}^{p} \theta_j^2 \qquad (20)$$

where λ is a hyperparameter that controls the strength of the regularization. This approach ensured that the model did not become overly complex, maintaining its ability to generalize.

Collaborative Research and Networking

Rowan also recognized the importance of collaboration in research. He actively sought out opportunities to work with fellow innovators and leading researchers in the field. This collaborative spirit was evident during a project aimed at improving image recognition systems. By pooling resources and knowledge, Rowan's team was able to develop a novel convolutional neural network (CNN) architecture that significantly outperformed existing models.

The architecture utilized multiple layers of convolutions, pooling, and activation functions, mathematically represented as:

$$Z = f(W * X + b) \qquad (21)$$

where Z is the output, W represents the weights, X is the input image, b is the bias term, and f is the activation function (such as ReLU). This collaborative effort not only enhanced Rowan's technical skills but also expanded his professional network, laying the groundwork for future endeavors.

Publications and Recognition

As Rowan immersed himself in AI research, his contributions did not go unnoticed. He authored several papers that were published in prestigious journals, garnering attention from both academia and industry. One of his most cited works focused on the ethical implications of AI in decision-making processes, a topic that resonated widely as the technology began to permeate various sectors.

Rowan's ability to articulate complex ideas with clarity and humor made him a sought-after speaker at conferences. His presentations often included anecdotes that highlighted the absurdities of AI, such as the time his model mistook a cat for a loaf of bread—an incident that left audiences in stitches while also prompting serious discussions about the limitations of current AI systems.

Conclusion

In conclusion, Rowan Levi's deep dive into AI research during his university years was characterized by a blend of rigorous theoretical exploration, hands-on project work, and collaborative networking. His experiences laid a solid foundation for his future contributions to the field, shaping him into the AI Whisperer he would become. With each breakthrough and challenge, Rowan not only advanced his understanding of machine learning but also prepared to tackle the ethical dilemmas and societal impacts that would come with the rise of AI technologies.

Collaboration with Fellow Future Innovators

Rowan Levi's time at the prestigious Ivy League university was not just a solitary journey of academic excellence; it was also characterized by a vibrant tapestry of collaboration with fellow innovators. In a world where the complexities of artificial intelligence (AI) and machine learning (ML) were rapidly evolving, the synergy of ideas among passionate peers proved to be a catalyst for groundbreaking advancements.

The Importance of Collaboration

Collaboration in the field of AI is essential for several reasons. Firstly, the interdisciplinary nature of AI necessitates inputs from diverse domains such as computer science, neuroscience, psychology, and ethics. This diversity leads to a more holistic approach to problem-solving. As Rowan often quipped, "If you're not collaborating, you're just talking to yourself, and let's be honest, that's a sign you need to get out more!"

Moreover, collaborative projects often yield more innovative solutions than solitary efforts. Research has shown that teams can outperform individuals in creative tasks due to the pooling of knowledge and ideas. For instance, a study by [?] found that collaborative brainstorming sessions led to a 30% increase in creative output compared to individual brainstorming.

Forming Alliances

During his university years, Rowan sought out fellow students who shared his fervor for AI. He formed alliances with a diverse group of peers, including computer science majors, cognitive science enthusiasts, and even philosophy students who brought ethical considerations to the table. This eclectic mix not only enriched discussions but also led to the development of innovative projects that combined various aspects of AI.

One notable project was a joint initiative aimed at improving natural language processing (NLP) algorithms. Collaborating with a linguistics major, Rowan and his team developed a model that could better understand context and nuance in human language. This project, titled *Contextual Understanding in NLP*, was later published in a leading academic journal, garnering attention for its innovative approach to language comprehension.

The Power of Hackathons

Hackathons became a significant part of Rowan's collaborative experience. These intense, time-limited events brought together students from different disciplines to tackle real-world problems using AI. At one memorable hackathon, Rowan and his team developed an AI-driven application that could predict mental health crises based on social media activity. The project not only won first place but also sparked discussions about the ethical implications of monitoring online behavior.

The experience at the hackathon highlighted several key theories in collaborative innovation. According to the *Innovation Diffusion Theory* [?], new ideas spread more rapidly when individuals from diverse backgrounds collaborate. Rowan's ability to engage with students from various fields exemplified this theory, as they combined their unique perspectives to create a product that was both innovative and socially relevant.

Mentorship and Guidance

Rowan's collaborations were not limited to peers; he also sought mentorship from established faculty members and industry professionals. These relationships were crucial in refining his ideas and gaining insights into the practical applications of his research. For instance, during a mentorship session with a renowned AI researcher, Rowan learned about the challenges of implementing machine learning algorithms in real-world scenarios, such as data bias and the importance of ethical considerations.

This mentorship experience led to the formation of a research group focused on ethical AI, where students could collaboratively explore the implications of their work. The group produced a white paper that outlined best practices for responsible AI development, which was later presented at an international conference. This initiative not only showcased the power of collaboration but also emphasized the need for ethical frameworks in the rapidly advancing field of AI.

Conclusion

Rowan Levi's university years were marked by an unwavering commitment to collaboration. His ability to connect with fellow innovators and engage in interdisciplinary projects not only enhanced his understanding of AI but also positioned him as a leader in the field. Through collaborative efforts, Rowan and his peers demonstrated that innovation is not a solitary endeavor; it thrives in an environment where diverse minds come together to challenge the status quo.

In the words of Rowan, "Collaboration is like a good AI model—it's all about the right inputs coming together to create something smarter than the sum of its parts." This philosophy would guide him throughout his career, as he continued to advocate for collaborative approaches in the ever-evolving landscape of artificial intelligence.

Internship at Prominent AI Company

During his university years, Rowan Levi secured an internship at a prominent AI company, TechNova, known for its cutting-edge advancements in artificial intelligence and machine learning. This internship was not just any summer gig; it was the golden ticket to the world of real-world applications of the theories he had been studying in the classroom.

The Application Process

Rowan's journey to TechNova began with a rigorous application process that included multiple interviews, coding challenges, and a presentation of his previous projects. He vividly remembers the coding challenge where he had to optimize a basic algorithm for sorting data. The challenge was to reduce the time complexity from $O(n^2)$ to $O(n \log n)$. After several sleepless nights, he finally implemented the QuickSort algorithm, which not only impressed the interviewers but also sparked a competitive fire within him.

Onboarding and Team Dynamics

Once accepted, Rowan went through an onboarding process that introduced him to the company's culture, mission, and the various teams working on AI projects. He was placed in the Natural Language Processing (NLP) team, where he was tasked with improving the company's existing chatbot technology. The team was a blend of seasoned professionals and fellow interns, creating a dynamic environment that encouraged collaboration and innovation.

Real-World Applications of NLP

Rowan's primary project involved enhancing the chatbot's ability to understand and respond to user queries more effectively. This required delving deep into various NLP techniques, such as tokenization, stemming, and the use of embeddings. One of the key algorithms he worked with was the Transformer model, introduced in the paper "Attention is All You Need" by Vaswani et al. (2017), which revolutionized the way machines process language.

The Transformer model utilizes a mechanism called self-attention, allowing the model to weigh the importance of different words in a sentence when making predictions. For example, in the sentence "The cat sat on the mat," the model learns to focus on the words "cat" and "mat" to understand the context better. This attention mechanism can be mathematically represented as:

$$\text{Attention}(Q, K, V) = \text{softmax}\left(\frac{QK^T}{\sqrt{d_k}}\right) V$$

where Q is the query, K is the key, V is the value, and d_k is the dimension of the keys.

Challenges Faced

Despite the excitement, the internship was not without its challenges. One significant hurdle was dealing with the chatbot's ability to handle ambiguous queries. For instance, when a user asked, "Can you book me a flight?" the chatbot often struggled to clarify the user's intent—whether they wanted a flight to a specific destination, a particular date, or even just general information about flight options.

To tackle this issue, Rowan proposed implementing a hierarchical classification system that first identified the type of query (e.g., booking, information request) before diving into more specific details. This approach improved the chatbot's accuracy significantly, leading to a 30% increase in successful query resolutions.

Mentorship and Learning

Throughout his internship, Rowan was fortunate to have a mentor, Dr. Sarah Chen, a leading figure in AI ethics and NLP. Dr. Chen guided him through the complexities of AI development, emphasizing the importance of ethical considerations in AI applications. She often reminded him, "Just because we can build it, doesn't mean we should." This mantra stuck with Rowan, shaping his views on the responsibilities of AI developers.

Impact on Career Trajectory

By the end of his internship, Rowan not only gained invaluable technical skills but also developed a deeper understanding of the ethical implications of AI technologies. His experience at TechNova solidified his decision to pursue a career in AI, particularly focusing on creating responsible and user-friendly applications.

In his final presentation to the team, Rowan showcased the improvements made to the chatbot, using metrics and visualizations to demonstrate its enhanced performance. The feedback was overwhelmingly positive, and he left the internship with a network of industry contacts and a renewed sense of purpose.

In conclusion, Rowan Levi's internship at TechNova was a pivotal moment in his journey as an AI innovator. It provided him with practical experience, mentorship, and a clearer vision of how he could contribute to the future of artificial intelligence. This experience would lay the groundwork for his subsequent breakthroughs and his commitment to ethical AI development.

Balancing Academics and Social Life

In the fast-paced environment of an Ivy League university, where the pressure to excel academically is as palpable as the aroma of overpriced coffee, Rowan Levi found himself navigating the treacherous waters of academic rigor and social engagement. The challenge of balancing these two facets of university life is a common struggle for many students, but for Rowan, it became a delicate dance that required both strategy and finesse.

The Challenge of Time Management

Time management is a critical skill that many students must master to succeed in both their studies and social lives. According to Covey's Time Management Matrix, tasks can be categorized into four quadrants based on their urgency and importance:

$$\text{Quadrant I: Urgent and Important} \quad \text{(Crisis management)} \quad (22)$$

$$\text{Quadrant II: Not Urgent but Important} \quad \text{(Planning and prevention)} \quad (23)$$

$$\text{Quadrant III: Urgent but Not Important} \quad \text{(Interruptions)} \quad (24)$$

$$\text{Quadrant IV: Not Urgent and Not Important} \quad \text{(Time wasters)} \quad (25)$$

Rowan learned to prioritize his tasks, focusing on Quadrant II activities that would contribute to his long-term goals in machine learning, while still making time for friends and social events that nourished his mental well-being.

Creating a Schedule

To maintain this balance, Rowan devised a weekly schedule that allocated specific blocks of time for studying, attending classes, and engaging in social activities. This schedule included:

- **Study Blocks:** Rowan dedicated evenings to studying, ensuring he was well-prepared for exams and projects. This included a mix of deep work sessions, where he would isolate himself from distractions, and collaborative study groups with peers.

- **Social Engagements:** He reserved weekends for social activities, from attending parties to participating in student organization events. This helped him recharge and connect with fellow students, which was crucial for maintaining his mental health.

- **Self-Care:** Recognizing the importance of self-care, Rowan scheduled time for exercise, mindfulness practices, and downtime. He often joked that he could code better after a good yoga session, as it helped clear his mind.

The Importance of Networking

In addition to maintaining a social life, Rowan understood the significance of networking within his academic environment. He attended various events, such as guest lectures and networking mixers, where he could meet industry professionals and fellow innovators. This dual approach of socializing and networking allowed him to build valuable connections that would benefit his career later on.

The Balancing Act: Real-Life Examples

Rowan's balancing act was not without its challenges. One notable incident occurred during midterms when he had a major project due alongside a friend's birthday party. Faced with the dilemma of choosing between academic responsibilities and social commitments, Rowan opted for a compromise:

- **Pre-Party Study Session:** He organized a study session with classmates before the party, ensuring that he was well-prepared for his project while still having time to celebrate with friends.

- **Shortened Attendance:** Rowan attended the party for a limited time, making a grand entrance and leaving early to finalize his project. His friends understood the demands of academia and appreciated his effort to balance both worlds.

This incident exemplified Rowan's ability to prioritize his responsibilities while still valuing his social life. He often joked that his friends were like his personal AI assistants, reminding him of important dates and deadlines.

Conclusion

Ultimately, Rowan Levi's experience in balancing academics and social life during his university years taught him invaluable lessons about time management, prioritization, and the importance of building relationships. By learning to navigate these challenges, he not only excelled in his studies but also cultivated a rich social life that supported his personal growth. This balance would later serve him well in his professional journey as the AI Whisperer, where the ability to connect with others and manage competing priorities became key components of his success.

Breakthroughs and Advancements

Groundbreaking Research in Natural Language Processing

Natural Language Processing (NLP) is a fascinating subfield of artificial intelligence that focuses on the interaction between computers and humans through natural language. Rowan Levi's groundbreaking research in NLP has not only advanced the field but also opened up new avenues for applications that were previously thought to be the stuff of science fiction.

Theoretical Foundations of NLP

At its core, NLP combines linguistics, computer science, and machine learning to enable machines to understand, interpret, and generate human language. The theoretical foundation of NLP can be traced back to several key concepts:

1. **Syntax and Semantics**: Syntax refers to the structure of sentences, while semantics deals with the meaning. Rowan's work often explores the balance between these two aspects, employing formal grammars to parse sentences and extract meaning.

2. **Statistical Models**: Traditional NLP relied heavily on rule-based systems. However, with the advent of statistical models, researchers began to leverage large corpora of text to train algorithms. This shift is exemplified by the

introduction of n-grams, which are contiguous sequences of n items from a given sample of text. For instance, the bigram model considers pairs of words, allowing the system to predict the next word based on the preceding one.

$$P(w_n|w_{n-1}) = \frac{C(w_{n-1}, w_n)}{C(w_{n-1})} \qquad (26)$$

where $P(w_n|w_{n-1})$ is the probability of word w_n given w_{n-1}, and C represents the count of occurrences.

3. **Deep Learning Techniques**: The introduction of deep learning has revolutionized NLP. Techniques such as Recurrent Neural Networks (RNNs) and Transformers have enabled models to capture long-range dependencies in text. The Transformer model, in particular, uses self-attention mechanisms to weigh the influence of different words in a sentence, allowing for a more nuanced understanding of context.

$$\text{Attention}(Q, K, V) = \text{softmax}\left(\frac{QK^T}{\sqrt{d_k}}\right) V \qquad (27)$$

where Q, K, and V represent the query, key, and value matrices, respectively, and d_k is the dimension of the key vectors.

Challenges in NLP

Despite significant advancements, NLP is not without its challenges. Rowan's research often addresses these issues head-on:

1. **Ambiguity**: Natural language is inherently ambiguous. Words can have multiple meanings (polysemy), and sentences can be structured in ways that lead to different interpretations. For example, the sentence "I saw the man with the telescope" can imply that either the speaker or the man possesses the telescope.

2. **Contextual Understanding**: Understanding context is crucial for accurate interpretation. Rowan's work on contextual embeddings, particularly with models like BERT (Bidirectional Encoder Representations from Transformers), has shown how context can drastically change the meaning of words based on their surrounding text.

3. **Low-Resource Languages**: Most NLP research has focused on high-resource languages like English, leaving many languages underrepresented. Rowan has advocated for techniques such as transfer learning, where knowledge gained while solving one problem is applied to a different but related problem, to address this gap.

Rowan's Contributions to NLP

Rowan Levi has made significant contributions to the field of NLP, particularly in the following areas:

1. **Sentiment Analysis**: Rowan developed a novel approach to sentiment analysis that utilizes deep learning to classify the emotional tone behind a series of words. By training models on diverse datasets, he was able to achieve state-of-the-art performance in identifying sentiments across various contexts, from product reviews to social media posts.

2. **Machine Translation**: Understanding the importance of accurate communication across languages, Rowan's research led to the development of a machine translation system that employs attention mechanisms to enhance translation quality. This system has been particularly effective in translating idiomatic expressions, which are often challenging for traditional models.

3. **Conversational Agents**: Rowan's work on conversational agents focuses on creating systems that can engage in natural, human-like dialogue. By integrating reinforcement learning techniques, he has developed chatbots that not only understand user intent but also learn from interactions, improving their responses over time.

Real-World Applications

The implications of Rowan's research extend far beyond academia. Some notable real-world applications include:

1. **Healthcare**: NLP technologies have been implemented in healthcare to analyze patient records and extract meaningful insights, aiding in diagnosis and treatment planning.

2. **Customer Service**: Many companies now utilize chatbots powered by Rowan's NLP advancements to handle customer inquiries, improving response times and customer satisfaction.

3. **Content Moderation**: Social media platforms have adopted NLP techniques to detect and filter harmful content, ensuring a safer online environment.

In conclusion, Rowan Levi's groundbreaking research in Natural Language Processing has not only advanced theoretical understanding but also facilitated practical applications that enhance everyday life. His contributions continue to shape the future of how humans and machines communicate, bridging the gap between technology and human language in ways that were once unimaginable.

Developing Highly Accurate Image Recognition Algorithm

Image recognition has become a cornerstone of artificial intelligence, enabling machines to interpret and understand visual data much like humans do. In this section, we explore Rowan Levi's groundbreaking work in developing a highly accurate image recognition algorithm that not only elevated his status in the tech community but also demonstrated the transformative power of machine learning in visual data interpretation.

Theoretical Foundations

The backbone of image recognition lies in convolutional neural networks (CNNs), a class of deep learning algorithms specifically designed for processing structured grid data, such as images. A CNN consists of multiple layers, including convolutional layers, pooling layers, and fully connected layers. The key equations that govern the operations of a convolutional layer can be expressed as follows:

$$Z = W * X + b \qquad (28)$$

Where: - Z is the output feature map, - W is the filter (or kernel), - X is the input image, - b is the bias term, and - $*$ denotes the convolution operation.

The convolution operation allows the network to learn spatial hierarchies of features, from simple edges and textures in the initial layers to complex shapes and objects in deeper layers.

Challenges in Image Recognition

Despite the theoretical advancements, developing a highly accurate image recognition algorithm comes with its own set of challenges:

- **Data Quality and Quantity:** The performance of image recognition algorithms is heavily dependent on the quality and quantity of the training data. Insufficient or biased datasets can lead to overfitting or underperformance in real-world applications.

- **Variability in Images:** Images can vary significantly due to factors such as lighting, angle, and occlusion. This variability can confuse the model, leading to misclassifications. For example, a cat might be misidentified as a dog if the image is taken from an unusual angle or in poor lighting conditions.

- **Computational Resources:** Training deep learning models, especially CNNs, requires substantial computational power and memory. Rowan faced the challenge of optimizing his algorithm to run efficiently on available hardware while maintaining accuracy.

- **Real-Time Processing:** For applications like autonomous vehicles or facial recognition, the algorithm must process images in real-time. This necessitates a balance between accuracy and speed, pushing the boundaries of current technology.

Rowan's Approach

Rowan Levi tackled these challenges with a multi-faceted approach:

- **Data Augmentation:** To enhance the diversity of the training dataset, Rowan employed data augmentation techniques. By applying transformations such as rotation, scaling, and flipping, he artificially increased the size of the dataset, helping the model generalize better to unseen images.

- **Transfer Learning:** Leveraging pre-trained models allowed Rowan to build on existing architectures that had already learned useful features from large datasets. By fine-tuning these models on his specific dataset, he achieved high accuracy with reduced training time.

- **Regularization Techniques:** To combat overfitting, Rowan implemented dropout and batch normalization techniques. Dropout randomly sets a fraction of the input units to zero during training, preventing the model from becoming overly reliant on specific features. Batch normalization helps stabilize learning by normalizing the inputs to each layer, allowing for higher learning rates and faster convergence.

- **Ensemble Methods:** Rowan also explored ensemble methods, combining multiple models to improve accuracy. By averaging the predictions of several different architectures, he reduced the likelihood of errors from any single model.

Results and Impact

Rowan's image recognition algorithm achieved remarkable results, setting a new benchmark in the field. He tested his model on a widely used dataset, the

CIFAR-10, which contains 60,000 images across 10 classes. The model achieved an accuracy of over 95%, significantly surpassing previous state-of-the-art results.

$$Accuracy = \frac{TP + TN}{TP + TN + FP + FN} \quad (29)$$

Where: - TP is the true positives, - TN is the true negatives, - FP is the false positives, and - FN is the false negatives.

The success of his algorithm led to its adoption in various applications, from medical imaging diagnostics to autonomous vehicle navigation, showcasing the versatility and potential of image recognition technology.

Conclusion

Rowan Levi's development of a highly accurate image recognition algorithm exemplifies the intersection of theoretical knowledge and practical application in artificial intelligence. By addressing the challenges of data quality, computational resources, and real-time processing, he not only advanced the field of machine learning but also paved the way for future innovations that leverage visual data in unprecedented ways. His work serves as a testament to the power of curiosity, perseverance, and a well-structured approach to problem-solving in the rapidly evolving landscape of technology.

Contributions to the Field of Reinforcement Learning

Reinforcement Learning (RL) has emerged as a pivotal area within the broader field of artificial intelligence, enabling machines to learn optimal behaviors through trial and error, much like humans. Rowan Levi's contributions to this domain have not only advanced theoretical understanding but also led to practical applications that have reshaped industries.

Understanding Reinforcement Learning

At its core, reinforcement learning involves an agent that interacts with an environment in order to maximize cumulative rewards. The agent learns from the consequences of its actions, adjusting its strategy based on feedback received from the environment. This process can be mathematically described by the Markov Decision Process (MDP), defined by the tuple (S, A, P, R, γ):

- S is the set of states.

- A is the set of actions.
- $P(s'|s,a)$ is the state transition probability, indicating the likelihood of moving to state s' from state s after taking action a.
- $R(s,a)$ is the reward received after taking action a in state s.
- γ is the discount factor, which balances immediate and future rewards.

The objective of the RL agent is to learn a policy $\pi : S \to A$ that maximizes the expected return G_t from time step t:

$$G_t = R_t + \gamma R_{t+1} + \gamma^2 R_{t+2} + \ldots$$

Key Contributions by Rowan Levi

Rowan Levi's work in reinforcement learning has centered around several groundbreaking contributions:

1. Development of Novel Algorithms One of Levi's significant contributions was the development of a novel algorithm that improved the efficiency of Q-learning, a fundamental RL algorithm. Traditional Q-learning updates the action-value function $Q(s,a)$ using the Bellman equation:

$$Q(s,a) \leftarrow Q(s,a) + \alpha[R + \gamma \max_{a'} Q(s',a') - Q(s,a)]$$

Levi introduced a method called Adaptive Q-Learning (AQL), which dynamically adjusts the learning rate α based on the variance of the rewards received. This approach allows for faster convergence in environments with high variability, making it particularly useful in real-world applications such as robotics and game playing.

2. Exploration-Exploitation Trade-off Another area of focus for Levi was the exploration-exploitation dilemma, which is crucial in RL. He proposed a hybrid strategy that combines epsilon-greedy methods with Upper Confidence Bound (UCB) techniques to balance exploration and exploitation more effectively. The updated policy can be expressed as:

$$a_t = \begin{cases} \text{random action} & \text{with probability } \epsilon \\ \arg\max_a Q(s_t, a) + c\sqrt{\frac{\ln n_t}{n_{t,a}}} & \text{with probability } 1 - \epsilon \end{cases}$$

where n_t is the total number of actions taken up to time t and $n_{t,a}$ is the number of times action a has been taken. This method not only enhances learning efficiency but also improves the agent's performance in complex environments.

3. Application in Real-World Scenarios Levi's research transcended theoretical advancements; he applied his algorithms in various real-world scenarios. One notable example was the implementation of his AQL algorithm in autonomous driving systems. By simulating various driving conditions, the system was able to learn optimal driving strategies while minimizing the risk of accidents. The results demonstrated a significant reduction in collision rates compared to traditional rule-based systems.

4. Ethical Considerations in RL Recognizing the potential ethical implications of reinforcement learning applications, Rowan Levi also contributed to discussions around responsible AI development. He advocated for the incorporation of ethical frameworks in RL algorithms, ensuring that agents not only maximize rewards but also adhere to societal norms and values. This perspective is crucial in applications such as healthcare and finance, where decisions can have profound impacts on human lives.

Conclusion

Rowan Levi's contributions to reinforcement learning have laid the groundwork for future innovations in AI. His algorithms and ethical considerations are paving the way for more intelligent, adaptable, and responsible AI systems. As the field continues to evolve, Levi's work will undoubtedly influence the trajectory of reinforcement learning and its applications across diverse industries.

Publications and Recognition in Academic Journals

Rowan Levi's journey into the world of machine learning was not just marked by his innovative projects and breakthroughs, but also by his prolific contributions to academic literature. By the time he reached his final years at university, Rowan had already established himself as a formidable voice in the field of artificial intelligence, with a string of publications that showcased his research prowess and unique insights.

Theoretical Contributions

Rowan's first major publication, titled *"Deep Learning for Natural Language Processing: A New Paradigm"*, co-authored with his mentor, Dr. Emily Chen, was published in the *Journal of Artificial Intelligence Research*. This paper delved into the transformative effects of deep learning architectures, such as Recurrent Neural Networks (RNNs) and Long Short-Term Memory (LSTM) networks, on the field of natural language processing (NLP). The authors posited that these models could significantly improve tasks such as sentiment analysis, machine translation, and text summarization.

The equation governing the LSTM model is given by:

$$f_t = \sigma(W_f \cdot [h_{t-1}, x_t] + b_f) \tag{30}$$

where f_t is the forget gate, W_f is the weight matrix, h_{t-1} is the previous hidden state, x_t is the input at time t, and b_f is the bias term. This foundational work not only garnered attention within academic circles but also laid the groundwork for subsequent research in NLP, earning Rowan recognition as a rising star in the AI community.

Addressing Contemporary Challenges

In another significant paper, *"Ethical Implications of Machine Learning in Automated Decision Making"*, Rowan tackled the pressing issue of bias in AI systems. Published in the *AI Ethics Journal*, this work examined how biased training data could lead to discriminatory outcomes in machine learning applications, particularly in hiring algorithms and credit scoring systems. He introduced the concept of *Fairness Constraints* to mitigate these biases, proposing the following optimization problem:

$$\min_{\theta} \mathcal{L}(\theta) + \lambda \cdot \text{Fairness}(\theta) \tag{31}$$

where $\mathcal{L}(\theta)$ is the loss function, λ is a regularization parameter, and $\text{Fairness}(\theta)$ quantifies the bias in the model's predictions. This publication not only received accolades for its relevance but also sparked a broader conversation about the ethical responsibilities of AI developers.

Innovations in Image Recognition

Rowan's contributions to image recognition were equally impressive. His paper, *"A Novel Approach to Image Classification Using Convolutional Neural Networks"*,

BREAKTHROUGHS AND ADVANCEMENTS

published in *Computer Vision and Image Understanding*, presented a new architecture that improved classification accuracy on standard datasets like CIFAR-10 and ImageNet. The architecture utilized a combination of convolutional layers, batch normalization, and dropout to enhance performance, leading to a significant reduction in overfitting.

The core of his model was expressed through the following convolutional operation:

$$Y[i,j] = \sum_m \sum_n X[i+m, j+n]K[m,n] \tag{32}$$

where Y is the output feature map, X is the input image, and K is the convolutional kernel. This work not only contributed to the academic literature but also caught the attention of tech giants looking to implement advanced image recognition systems.

Recognition and Awards

Rowan's publications did not go unnoticed. His work led to several awards, including the prestigious *Best Paper Award* at the International Conference on Machine Learning (ICML) for his co-authored paper on reinforcement learning titled *"Exploration Strategies in Reinforcement Learning: A Comparative Study"*. This paper provided a comprehensive analysis of various exploration strategies, such as ⊠-greedy and Upper Confidence Bound (UCB), and their impact on learning efficiency. The equation representing the UCB strategy is given by:

$$a_t = \arg\max_a \left(\hat{Q}(a) + c\sqrt{\frac{\ln t}{N(a)}} \right) \tag{33}$$

where $\hat{Q}(a)$ is the estimated value of action a, c is a constant, t is the total number of trials, and $N(a)$ is the number of times action a has been selected. This paper not only solidified Rowan's status as an innovator but also influenced future research in reinforcement learning.

Impact on Academia and Industry

Rowan's publications have had a lasting impact not only in academia but also in industry. His research has been cited extensively, influencing both theoretical advancements and practical applications in various domains, from healthcare AI to autonomous vehicles. His ability to bridge the gap between complex theoretical concepts and real-world applications has made him a sought-after speaker at conferences and workshops, where he shares his insights on the future of AI.

In summary, Rowan Levi's contributions to academic journals were characterized by a blend of theoretical depth, practical relevance, and ethical considerations. His works not only advanced the field of machine learning but also set the stage for future innovators to build upon his findings, ensuring that his legacy would endure long after his university years.

Speaker at AI Conferences and Events

Rowan Levi's rise to prominence in the field of artificial intelligence was not just due to his groundbreaking research but also his ability to articulate complex concepts to a broader audience. As a speaker at various AI conferences and events, Rowan became known for his engaging presentations that combined humor, insightful commentary, and deep technical knowledge.

The Importance of Conferences in AI

AI conferences serve as crucial platforms for researchers, industry leaders, and enthusiasts to gather, share knowledge, and foster collaboration. They provide an opportunity to discuss the latest advancements, showcase innovative projects, and address pressing ethical concerns in the rapidly evolving field of AI. Rowan recognized the significance of these gatherings early in his career and made it a point to participate actively.

Keynote Speeches and Panels

Rowan's keynote speeches often drew large crowds, where he tackled topics such as the future of machine learning, ethical AI, and the societal implications of automation. For instance, during his keynote at the International Conference on Machine Learning (ICML), he presented a compelling argument on the need for transparency in AI systems. He famously quipped, "If we can't understand how our algorithms make decisions, we might as well be consulting a magic 8-ball!" This humorous analogy not only entertained the audience but also emphasized a critical point in AI ethics.

In addition to keynotes, Rowan frequently participated in panel discussions. His ability to engage in spirited debates with other leading AI experts made him a sought-after panelist. One memorable panel at the NeurIPS conference revolved around the potential job displacement caused by AI. Rowan argued that while automation might replace certain jobs, it would also create new opportunities, saying, "If robots take your job, don't worry! They'll need someone to teach them how to make coffee!"

Workshops and Tutorials

Rowan also conducted hands-on workshops, where he guided participants through the intricacies of machine learning algorithms. His workshop on "Building Your First Neural Network" became particularly popular among students and young professionals. He used real-world datasets to illustrate concepts, demonstrating how to train a model using the popular TensorFlow library. The workshop culminated in a friendly competition where participants created their models to predict housing prices, with Rowan playfully awarding the winner a "Golden Neural Network" trophy—a golden spray-painted coffee mug.

Engaging with Diverse Audiences

Understanding that AI affects a wide range of sectors, Rowan tailored his presentations to engage diverse audiences. Whether speaking to tech-savvy engineers or policymakers with limited technical backgrounds, he adapted his language and examples accordingly. For instance, during a talk at a tech policy summit, he explained reinforcement learning using a relatable analogy: "Imagine teaching your dog to fetch. You reward him with treats when he brings the ball back. That's reinforcement learning in a nutshell—minus the slobber!"

Impact on the AI Community

Rowan's presence at these events helped demystify AI for many. His approachable demeanor and willingness to answer questions fostered an inclusive environment, encouraging young innovators to explore the field. He often emphasized the importance of collaboration, stating, "We are all in this together. AI is not just about algorithms; it's about people, ideas, and the impact we can make collectively."

Conclusion

Through his engaging speaking style and commitment to outreach, Rowan Levi not only established himself as a thought leader in the AI community but also inspired countless individuals to pursue careers in technology. His contributions to conferences and events have left a lasting impact, proving that effective communication is just as crucial as technical expertise in the field of artificial intelligence.

$$\text{Impact} = \text{Engagement} \times \text{Knowledge Sharing} \qquad (34)$$

Rise to Prominence

Industry Recognition and Job Offers

Engaging with Leading Tech Companies

As Rowan Levi emerged as a prominent figure in the field of artificial intelligence, his journey took a decisive turn when he began engaging with leading tech companies. This phase of his career was not only about securing job offers but also about creating meaningful partnerships that would push the boundaries of what AI could achieve.

Rowan's approach to engaging with these companies was akin to a well-crafted algorithm—strategic, efficient, and results-oriented. He understood that in the tech industry, relationships are as crucial as the technology itself. To illustrate this, let's break down the key components of his engagement strategy:

Identifying Potential Partners

Rowan meticulously researched leading tech companies that were at the forefront of AI innovation. Companies like Google, Microsoft, and IBM were on his radar, not just for their technological prowess but also for their commitment to ethical AI practices. He analyzed their recent projects, focusing on how they aligned with his own vision for responsible AI development.

$$\text{Engagement Score} = \frac{\text{Innovation Level} + \text{Ethical Standards}}{\text{Market Competition}} \qquad (35)$$

This equation encapsulated his thought process; he sought partnerships where innovation was high, ethical standards were prioritized, and competition was manageable.

Networking and Building Relationships

Rowan leveraged his academic connections, attending conferences and workshops where industry leaders gathered. He was not just a passive attendee; he actively participated in discussions, presenting his research on natural language processing and machine learning. His ability to articulate complex concepts in an accessible manner made him a sought-after speaker.

His networking efforts often led to serendipitous encounters. For instance, at a tech summit, he met a senior researcher from Google who was impressed by Rowan's work on reinforcement learning algorithms. This encounter eventually led to a collaborative project that enhanced Google's AI capabilities in real-time data processing.

Tailoring Proposals to Industry Needs

Understanding the specific needs of each tech company was crucial. Rowan crafted tailored proposals that addressed the pain points of potential partners. For example, he identified that many companies struggled with the integration of AI into their existing systems.

$$\text{Proposal Effectiveness} = \frac{\text{Alignment with Company Needs}}{\text{Complexity of Implementation}} \qquad (36)$$

Rowan aimed to maximize this effectiveness ratio by ensuring that his proposals were not only innovative but also feasible. His project aimed at developing a user-friendly interface for AI tools became a game-changer for several companies, allowing them to adopt AI solutions without overhauling their entire infrastructure.

Showcasing Results and Building Credibility

Once engaged, Rowan made it a point to showcase tangible results from his collaborations. He understood that in tech, results speak louder than words. By quantifying the impact of his work, such as improvements in efficiency or accuracy in AI applications, he built credibility within the industry.

For instance, his work on an image recognition algorithm led to a 30% increase in accuracy for a major retail company's inventory management system. This success story circulated within industry circles, leading to further opportunities.

Navigating Challenges and Ethical Considerations

Despite the successes, engaging with leading tech companies also presented challenges. Rowan faced ethical dilemmas regarding data privacy and the potential misuse of AI technologies. He was vocal about these concerns, advocating for transparency and responsible AI practices in all collaborations.

$$\text{Ethical AI Score} = \frac{\text{Transparency} + \text{User Consent}}{\text{Data Utilization}} \qquad (37)$$

He sought to maintain a high Ethical AI Score in all his projects, ensuring that user consent was prioritized and that data utilization was transparent. This commitment not only distinguished him in the tech landscape but also attracted like-minded companies eager to collaborate on ethical AI initiatives.

Conclusion

Engaging with leading tech companies was a pivotal aspect of Rowan Levi's career. His strategic approach, characterized by thorough research, relationship-building, tailored proposals, and a commitment to ethical practices, set him apart as a thought leader in the AI community. As he continued to navigate this dynamic landscape, his influence grew, shaping the future of AI in ways that were both innovative and responsible.

The AI Whisperer's Unique Approach

Rowan Levi, known in the tech world as the "AI Whisperer," has carved a niche for himself through his unconventional and innovative approach to machine learning. Unlike many of his contemporaries who focus solely on algorithmic advancements, Rowan emphasizes a holistic understanding of AI, combining technical prowess with a deep appreciation for human-centered design. This section explores the unique aspects of Rowan's methodology, highlighting the theoretical frameworks he employs, the challenges he addresses, and illustrative examples of his work.

Human-Centric AI Design

At the core of Rowan's approach is the principle of human-centric AI design. He believes that technology should not only serve efficiency but also enhance the human experience. This perspective is rooted in the theories of participatory design, where end-users are actively involved in the design process. Rowan often states, "If your AI doesn't understand people, it's just a fancy calculator."

To implement this, he employs techniques such as user interviews, ethnographic studies, and co-design workshops, ensuring that the voices of diverse user groups are heard. For instance, when developing a natural language processing (NLP) tool for mental health support, Rowan gathered insights from psychologists, patients, and tech developers to create an AI that genuinely understands emotional nuances. This approach led to a system that not only provides accurate responses but also offers empathetic interactions, significantly improving user satisfaction.

Interdisciplinary Collaboration

Rowan's unique approach also emphasizes interdisciplinary collaboration. He recognizes that the challenges posed by AI cannot be solved by technologists alone; hence, he actively seeks partnerships with experts from various fields, including ethics, sociology, and psychology. This collaboration is grounded in the theory of transdisciplinary research, which advocates for the integration of knowledge across disciplines to address complex societal problems.

For example, during a project aimed at developing an AI system for predictive policing, Rowan partnered with criminologists and community activists. This collaboration led to a more nuanced understanding of the societal implications of AI in law enforcement, resulting in a system designed to assist rather than surveil. By incorporating social insights, Rowan's team was able to mitigate potential biases in the algorithms, a common problem in AI applications.

Ethical AI Development

Rowan's commitment to ethical AI development sets him apart from many in the field. He believes that with great power comes great responsibility, and this mantra drives his work. He often references the ethical frameworks proposed by scholars like Nick Bostrom and Kate Crawford, which highlight the potential risks of AI, including bias, discrimination, and loss of privacy.

In practice, Rowan implements rigorous ethical review processes for all his projects. For instance, when developing an AI-driven hiring tool, he ensured that the algorithm was rigorously tested for biases against gender and ethnicity. By employing techniques such as adversarial testing, where the AI is challenged with edge cases to identify biases, Rowan's team was able to refine the model, ensuring fairness in hiring practices.

Continuous Learning and Adaptation

Another hallmark of Rowan's approach is his emphasis on continuous learning and adaptation. He believes that AI systems should evolve alongside society, adapting to new data and changing human needs. This is aligned with the principles of lifelong learning in AI, where models are designed to improve over time.

Rowan often cites the example of his work on an AI recommendation system for educational platforms. By incorporating feedback loops and user interaction data, the system continuously learns from user behavior, refining its recommendations to better suit individual learning styles. This adaptability not only enhances user engagement but also ensures that the AI remains relevant in a rapidly changing educational landscape.

Emphasis on Transparency

Lastly, transparency is a cornerstone of Rowan's unique approach. He advocates for explainable AI, where users can understand how decisions are made by the AI systems they interact with. This is crucial in building trust, particularly in applications that significantly impact lives, such as healthcare and finance.

Rowan's team developed a visualization tool that allows users to see the decision-making process of their AI systems. For example, in a healthcare application that predicts patient outcomes, users can view the factors that influenced the AI's recommendations. This transparency not only empowers users but also facilitates informed decision-making, aligning with ethical principles of autonomy and informed consent.

Conclusion

In summary, Rowan Levi's unique approach to machine learning transcends traditional boundaries, integrating human-centric design, interdisciplinary collaboration, ethical considerations, continuous learning, and transparency. By doing so, he not only advances the field of AI but also ensures that technology serves humanity in a meaningful way. His work exemplifies the potential of AI when guided by a thoughtful and comprehensive methodology, setting a standard for future innovators in the tech landscape.

$$AI_{\text{human-centric}} = \text{Technology} + \text{Empathy} + \text{Collaboration} \tag{38}$$

Big Breakthroughs in Industrial Applications of AI

Rowan Levi, dubbed the "AI Whisperer," made significant strides in the industrial applications of artificial intelligence. His work not only transformed businesses but also set new standards for efficiency and innovation. This subsection delves into some of the most notable breakthroughs that emerged during his rise to prominence.

Predictive Maintenance in Manufacturing

One of Rowan's most impactful contributions was in the realm of predictive maintenance for manufacturing equipment. Traditional maintenance schedules often lead to either excessive downtime or unnecessary costs. By leveraging machine learning algorithms, Rowan developed a predictive model that analyzed real-time data from machinery sensors.

The predictive maintenance model can be represented mathematically as follows:

$$P(M_t) = f(X_t, \theta) \tag{39}$$

where $P(M_t)$ is the probability of machine failure at time t, X_t represents the features extracted from sensor data, and θ are the parameters learned during training.

This approach allowed companies to foresee equipment failures before they occurred, reducing downtime by up to 30% and saving millions in repair costs. For example, a leading automotive manufacturer implemented Rowan's model and reported a 25% increase in production efficiency within the first year.

Supply Chain Optimization

Rowan also revolutionized supply chain management through AI-driven optimization techniques. By employing reinforcement learning algorithms, he designed a system that dynamically adjusted inventory levels based on real-time demand forecasts. The mathematical framework for this optimization can be expressed as:

$$\text{Maximize } E[R] = \sum_{t=1}^{T} \gamma^{t-1} r_t \tag{40}$$

where $E[R]$ is the expected return, r_t is the reward at time t, and γ is the discount factor.

This system not only minimized excess inventory but also improved customer satisfaction by ensuring product availability. A major retail chain that adopted this approach saw a 15% reduction in holding costs and a 20% improvement in order fulfillment rates.

Quality Control with Computer Vision

In the realm of quality control, Rowan's advancements in computer vision technology significantly enhanced product inspection processes. By training convolutional neural networks (CNNs) on large datasets of product images, he created a system capable of detecting defects with unprecedented accuracy. The performance of a CNN can be described by the following equation:

$$y = f(W * x + b) \tag{41}$$

where y is the output, W represents the weights of the network, x is the input image, and b is the bias term.

Implementing this technology in a consumer electronics factory resulted in a 40% decrease in defective products reaching the market. This not only saved costs related to returns and repairs but also enhanced the brand's reputation for quality.

AI-Driven Customer Service Solutions

Rowan also pioneered the development of AI-driven customer service solutions that utilized natural language processing (NLP) to enhance user experience. By creating chatbots capable of understanding and responding to customer inquiries in real-time, companies were able to reduce response times significantly. The underlying NLP model can be represented as:

$$P(w|h) = \frac{P(h|w)P(w)}{P(h)} \tag{42}$$

where $P(w|h)$ is the probability of word w given history h.

One telecommunications company that integrated Rowan's chatbot technology reported a 50% reduction in customer service costs and a 70% increase in customer satisfaction scores. This transformation showcased the potential of AI to enhance user interactions while reducing the burden on human agents.

Energy Management Systems

Lastly, Rowan's contributions to energy management systems through AI algorithms have been transformative for industries looking to reduce their carbon footprint. By employing predictive analytics and optimization techniques, he developed models that forecast energy consumption patterns and suggest optimal energy usage strategies. The optimization problem can be expressed as:

$$\min \sum_{t=1}^{T} C_t \cdot E_t \qquad (43)$$

where C_t is the cost of energy at time t and E_t is the energy consumption.

A large manufacturing firm that implemented Rowan's energy management system achieved a 20% reduction in energy costs while simultaneously lowering its greenhouse gas emissions. This not only benefited the company's bottom line but also positioned it as a leader in sustainable practices.

Conclusion

Rowan Levi's breakthroughs in industrial applications of AI exemplify the profound impact of machine learning on various sectors. From predictive maintenance to energy management, his innovative solutions have not only optimized operations but also paved the way for a more sustainable future. As industries continue to embrace AI, Rowan's legacy as the "AI Whisperer" will undoubtedly resonate, inspiring future innovators to push the boundaries of what is possible with technology.

Collaborations with Renowned Scientists and Innovators

Rowan Levi's ascent in the field of artificial intelligence was not solely due to his individual brilliance; it was significantly bolstered by his strategic collaborations with some of the most esteemed scientists and innovators in the AI community. Recognizing that innovation often springs from the intersection of diverse ideas, Rowan sought partnerships that combined expertise across various domains of technology.

One of his most notable collaborations was with Dr. Aisha Patel, a leading figure in the field of Natural Language Processing (NLP). Together, they embarked on a project aimed at improving sentiment analysis algorithms, which had become increasingly crucial in understanding consumer behavior. The primary challenge they faced was the ambiguity of human language, which can often lead to misinterpretations by AI systems. As articulated in their joint paper, *Contextual Sentiment Analysis: A New Paradigm*, they proposed a novel approach that utilized contextual embeddings to enhance the accuracy of sentiment detection. The foundational equation of their model can be represented as follows:

$$S = \sum_{i=1}^{n} w_i \cdot e_{context}(x_i) \quad (44)$$

where S is the sentiment score, w_i represents the weight of the word x_i, and $e_{context}(x_i)$ is the contextual embedding of the word based on its surrounding text. This collaboration not only led to significant advancements in NLP but also garnered recognition at major AI conferences, solidifying Rowan's reputation as a thought leader in the field.

In addition to his work with Dr. Patel, Rowan also collaborated with Dr. Marcus Chen, an expert in reinforcement learning. Their joint initiative focused on developing an advanced algorithm for autonomous navigation in robotics. The problem they aimed to solve was the inefficiency of traditional reinforcement learning approaches in dynamic environments. By implementing a novel approach that integrated deep learning with reinforcement learning, they were able to create a more adaptable algorithm. This was encapsulated in the following optimization problem:

$$\max_{\pi} \mathbb{E}\left[\sum_{t=0}^{T} \gamma^t R(s_t, a_t)\right] \quad (45)$$

where π is the policy, $R(s_t, a_t)$ is the reward function at time t, and γ is the discount factor. Their work culminated in a breakthrough paper that proposed a hybrid model, which significantly outperformed previous benchmarks in simulated environments.

Rowan's collaborations extended beyond academia. He partnered with industry leaders, including a startup focused on AI-driven healthcare solutions. This collaboration aimed to leverage machine learning to predict patient outcomes based on historical data. The challenge was to ensure the model's interpretability while maintaining high accuracy. Through joint efforts, they developed a framework that utilized explainable AI techniques, allowing healthcare professionals to understand the decision-making process of the AI. The framework was grounded in the following principles:

$$\text{Interpretability} = f(\text{Accuracy}, \text{Transparency}) \quad (46)$$

This equation highlights the trade-off between accuracy and transparency, a critical consideration in healthcare applications. Their work was recognized with an award for innovation in medical technology, further establishing Rowan's reputation as a pioneering collaborator.

Moreover, Rowan's ability to foster relationships with innovators across disciplines was exemplified by his participation in hackathons and collaborative workshops. He often emphasized the importance of interdisciplinary teamwork, stating, "AI is not just about algorithms; it's about understanding the human experience." This perspective led him to collaborate with artists and social scientists, exploring the ethical implications of AI in society. One such project involved creating an interactive installation that showcased the impact of AI on daily life, blending art with technology to provoke thought and discussion.

In summary, Rowan Levi's collaborations with renowned scientists and innovators were instrumental in propelling his career and advancing the field of AI. By embracing diversity in thought and expertise, he not only contributed to groundbreaking research but also fostered a culture of collaboration that continues to inspire future generations of innovators. His partnerships serve as a reminder that in the rapidly evolving landscape of technology, collaboration is not just beneficial; it is essential for meaningful progress.

Establishing Himself as a Thought Leader

Rowan Levi's rise as a thought leader in the rapidly evolving field of artificial intelligence (AI) is a testament to his innovative contributions and his ability to engage with complex societal issues surrounding technology. As he transitioned from academia to industry, Rowan recognized that being at the forefront of technological advancements also meant taking on the mantle of responsibility. This realization was pivotal in shaping his approach to AI, both in terms of technical innovation and ethical considerations.

The Intersection of Innovation and Ethics

In the early stages of his career, Rowan was acutely aware of the ethical implications of AI technologies. He often cited the work of prominent philosophers like Nick Bostrom, who discussed the potential existential risks associated with advanced AI systems. Bostrom's framework for understanding AI safety, particularly the concept of *superintelligence*, provided a foundation for Rowan's advocacy. He believed that as AI systems became more capable, the need for responsible governance and ethical oversight would become increasingly critical.

Rowan frequently referenced the equation for *utility maximization* in AI systems:

$$U(a) = \sum_{s \in S} P(s|a) \cdot V(s) \tag{47}$$

where $U(a)$ is the utility of action a, $P(s|a)$ is the probability of state s given action a, and $V(s)$ is the value of state s. This equation underscored the importance of designing AI that not only maximizes efficiency but also aligns with human values and ethical standards.

Public Engagement and Thought Leadership

To establish himself as a thought leader, Rowan leveraged various platforms to communicate his insights on AI. He became a sought-after speaker at international conferences, where he shared his research findings and engaged in discussions about the future of AI. His presentations often included interactive elements, such as live demonstrations of his machine learning models, which captivated audiences and fostered deeper understanding.

Rowan's TED Talks, particularly one titled *"AI for Good: Balancing Innovation with Responsibility"*, garnered significant attention. In this talk, he highlighted the potential of AI to address pressing global challenges, such as climate change and healthcare disparities, while emphasizing the importance of ethical considerations. He famously quipped, "If we can teach machines to learn from our mistakes, why can't we teach ourselves to learn from theirs?" This humorous yet poignant statement resonated with audiences, making complex topics more accessible.

Collaborations and Influence

Rowan's influence extended beyond public speaking; he actively collaborated with other thought leaders in the tech industry. He partnered with organizations like the Partnership on AI, where he contributed to discussions on best practices for AI development. His collaborative projects often focused on creating frameworks for ethical AI that could be adopted by companies worldwide.

An example of this was his involvement in the development of the *AI Ethics Guidelines*, which aimed to provide a comprehensive set of principles for responsible AI use. These guidelines emphasized transparency, accountability, and inclusivity, advocating for diverse voices in AI development. Rowan's commitment to these principles established him as a credible figure in the discourse surrounding ethical AI.

Media Presence and Publications

Recognizing the power of media in shaping public perception, Rowan also cultivated a strong online presence. He authored articles for reputable publications, such as *Wired* and *MIT Technology Review*, where he discussed the implications of

AI advancements. His writing style, infused with humor and relatable anecdotes, made complex concepts digestible for a broader audience.

In one article, he humorously compared the unpredictability of AI algorithms to a toddler with a crayon: "You never know when they might create a masterpiece or just draw all over the walls." This analogy not only entertained but also highlighted the unpredictable nature of machine learning models, emphasizing the need for careful oversight.

Conclusion

Through a combination of innovative research, public engagement, and ethical advocacy, Rowan Levi successfully established himself as a thought leader in the field of AI. His unique approach, characterized by a blend of technical expertise and a commitment to responsible AI development, positioned him as a key figure in shaping the future of technology. As he continued to navigate the complexities of AI, Rowan remained dedicated to fostering a dialogue that balanced innovation with ethical considerations, ensuring that the machines of tomorrow would serve humanity's best interests.

Ethical Considerations and Public Debate

AI's Impact on Employment and Human Rights

The integration of Artificial Intelligence (AI) into various sectors has sparked a heated debate regarding its impact on employment and human rights. As Rowan Levi, the AI Whisperer, navigates this complex landscape, he finds himself at the forefront of discussions that challenge the very fabric of labor markets and the ethical considerations surrounding AI technologies.

The Automation Dilemma

One of the most pressing concerns regarding AI is its potential to automate jobs, leading to displacement of workers. According to a study by [?], it is estimated that nearly 47% of jobs in the United States are at risk of being automated within the next two decades. This projection raises critical questions about the future of work and the economic structures that support it.

To illustrate, consider the manufacturing sector, where robots have already replaced many manual labor jobs. For instance, the introduction of AI-driven robotic arms has increased efficiency but has also led to significant job losses among assembly line workers. The equation governing this relationship can be summarized as:

$$\text{Job Loss} = f(\text{Automation Level}, \text{Industry Adaptation Rate})$$

Where f represents the function that correlates the level of automation with the rate at which industries adapt to new technologies.

The Skills Gap

As AI technologies evolve, there is an increasing demand for a workforce equipped with advanced technical skills. This phenomenon has created a skills gap, where the existing workforce may not possess the necessary qualifications to thrive in an AI-driven economy. Rowan advocates for educational reforms to address this gap, emphasizing the need for STEM (Science, Technology, Engineering, and Mathematics) education.

The skills gap can be represented by the following inequality:

$$\text{Skills Required} > \text{Skills Available}$$

This inequality highlights the urgency of upskilling and reskilling initiatives. Without such measures, marginalized communities may face even greater challenges in accessing employment opportunities, exacerbating existing inequalities.

Ethical Considerations in AI Deployment

The deployment of AI technologies raises significant ethical concerns, particularly regarding human rights. Issues such as surveillance, data privacy, and algorithmic bias are at the forefront of discussions. For instance, facial recognition technology has been criticized for its disproportionate impact on minority groups, leading to wrongful accusations and violations of privacy rights.

Rowan emphasizes the importance of responsible AI development, advocating for transparency in algorithms and inclusivity in data collection. The ethical framework can be summarized as:

$$\text{Ethical AI} = \text{Transparency} + \text{Accountability} + \text{Inclusivity}$$

This equation serves as a guiding principle for AI practitioners and policymakers alike, ensuring that technological advancements do not come at the expense of fundamental human rights.

Case Studies and Real-World Implications

Several case studies exemplify the impact of AI on employment and human rights. For instance, the implementation of AI in the hiring process has raised concerns over bias and discrimination. A notable example is Amazon's AI recruiting tool, which was found to favor male candidates over female candidates due to biased training data. This incident underscores the need for rigorous testing and evaluation of AI systems to prevent perpetuating existing biases.

Moreover, the gig economy, driven by AI platforms, has transformed traditional employment models. While it offers flexibility, it also raises questions about workers' rights and job security. Gig workers often lack access to benefits such as healthcare and retirement plans, creating a precarious employment landscape.

The Path Forward

As Rowan Levi navigates the challenges posed by AI's impact on employment and human rights, he advocates for a multi-faceted approach that includes:

- **Policy Advocacy:** Engaging with policymakers to create regulations that protect workers' rights in the face of automation.

- **Education and Training:** Promoting initiatives that equip individuals with the skills necessary to thrive in an AI-driven economy.

- **Ethical Standards:** Establishing ethical guidelines for AI development and deployment to safeguard human rights.

In conclusion, while AI presents opportunities for innovation and efficiency, it also poses significant challenges that must be addressed. Rowan Levi's commitment to responsible AI development underscores the importance of balancing technological advancements with the protection of human rights and the promotion of equitable employment opportunities.

Rowan Levi's Advocacy for Responsible AI Development

In an era where artificial intelligence (AI) is rapidly evolving, Rowan Levi has emerged as a prominent advocate for responsible AI development. His advocacy is grounded in the understanding that while AI has the potential to revolutionize industries and improve lives, it also poses significant ethical challenges that must be addressed to ensure its benefits are realized equitably.

Theoretical Framework

Rowan's approach is informed by several key theories in AI ethics, including the principles of fairness, accountability, and transparency (FAT). These principles serve as a guiding framework for his work, emphasizing that AI systems should be designed and implemented in ways that are just and understandable.

$$\text{Fairness} = \frac{\text{Number of Unbiased Outcomes}}{\text{Total Outcomes}} \qquad (48)$$

This equation illustrates that fairness in AI can be quantitatively assessed by the ratio of unbiased outcomes to total outcomes. Rowan argues that achieving fairness requires rigorous testing and validation of AI algorithms to identify and mitigate biases that could lead to discriminatory practices.

Identifying Problems

One of the primary problems that Rowan seeks to address is algorithmic bias, which occurs when AI systems produce results that are systematically prejudiced due to erroneous assumptions in the machine learning process. For instance, a study by Angwin et al. (2016) revealed that a predictive policing algorithm disproportionately targeted minority communities, leading to a cycle of over-policing and community mistrust.

Rowan highlights that such biases often stem from historical data that reflect societal prejudices. He asserts that without careful consideration of the data used to train AI systems, we risk perpetuating and amplifying existing inequalities. To combat this, he advocates for diverse datasets that accurately represent the populations affected by AI decisions.

Real-World Examples

To illustrate the importance of responsible AI development, Rowan often references the case of facial recognition technology, which has been shown to misidentify individuals from certain demographic groups at significantly higher rates. A study conducted by Buolamwini and Gebru (2018) revealed that commercial facial recognition systems had an error rate of 34.7% for darker-skinned women compared to just 0.8% for lighter-skinned men.

Rowan argues that these disparities are not merely technical failures but ethical failures that can have real-world consequences, such as wrongful arrests or exclusion from services. He emphasizes the need for developers to implement bias audits and fairness assessments as standard practices in the development lifecycle of AI technologies.

Advocacy Initiatives

In his advocacy efforts, Rowan has launched several initiatives aimed at promoting responsible AI. One notable program is the "AI for All" campaign, which seeks to educate stakeholders about the ethical implications of AI and encourage the adoption of best practices in AI development. This initiative includes workshops, online courses, and community outreach programs designed to empower individuals from underrepresented backgrounds to engage with AI technology critically.

Moreover, Rowan actively collaborates with policymakers to shape regulations that govern AI deployment. He believes that clear guidelines and standards are essential for ensuring that AI technologies are developed and used in ways that prioritize human rights and dignity.

Public Speaking and Engagements

Rowan's commitment to responsible AI has led him to become a sought-after speaker at international conferences and panels. During his TED Talks, he passionately discusses the societal implications of AI, urging technologists to consider the broader impact of their innovations. His engaging delivery often includes humor and relatable anecdotes, making complex ethical discussions accessible to diverse audiences.

In one memorable talk, he quipped, "If your AI can't tell the difference between a cat and a dog, how can we trust it to make decisions about our lives?" This light-hearted approach helps demystify AI while driving home the importance of accountability in its development.

Conclusion

Rowan Levi's advocacy for responsible AI development is not just a professional endeavor; it is a moral imperative. By championing fairness, accountability, and transparency, he aims to create a future where AI serves as a force for good, enhancing human capabilities rather than undermining them. His efforts remind us that as we advance technologically, we must also evolve ethically, ensuring that the innovations we create reflect our shared values and aspirations for a just society.

Through his work, Rowan Levi continues to inspire a new generation of innovators to prioritize ethical considerations in their pursuits, fostering a culture of responsibility in the ever-evolving field of artificial intelligence.

Public Speaking Engagements and TED Talks

Rowan Levi, often referred to as the "AI Whisperer," didn't just stop at developing groundbreaking algorithms; he took his talents to the stage, captivating audiences with his charisma and knowledge. If you've ever attended a tech conference and felt your brain melting from jargon overload, you know how essential it is to have someone like Rowan at the helm.

The Art of Storytelling

Rowan understood that the key to effective public speaking is not just to inform but to entertain. Channeling his inner Ali Wong, he often began his talks with a personal anecdote that would have the audience roaring with laughter. For instance, during his first TED Talk titled "From Algorithms to Empathy," he shared the story of how his first AI project was so bad it could barely recognize his cat, Fluffy, as anything more than a "slightly confused potato."

This approach not only made complex ideas accessible but also humanized the often sterile world of artificial intelligence. He would seamlessly transition from humorous tales to serious discussions about the implications of AI in everyday life, much like how one might go from discussing the latest Netflix series to the existential threat of machines taking over the world.

Key Topics and Theories

During his engagements, Rowan delved into several key topics that resonated with both tech enthusiasts and the general public. One of his favorite theories to discuss was the concept of **Machine Learning Bias**, which he explained using a relatable analogy:

> "Imagine teaching a child to identify fruits. If you only show them apples and oranges, they might think that bananas are just elongated oranges. This is the same way algorithms can develop biases based on the data they are trained on."

He would then illustrate this problem with real-world examples, such as facial recognition software misidentifying people of color, emphasizing the urgent need for diverse datasets in training AI systems.

Engagements and Collaborations

Rowan's public speaking engagements weren't limited to TED Talks. He became a regular at industry conferences, universities, and even community centers, where he made it a point to reach out to underrepresented groups in tech. He believed that if AI was to serve humanity, it should be developed by a diverse set of minds.

One of his notable collaborations was with the **Tech for All** initiative, where he spoke about the importance of inclusivity in technology. His sessions often included interactive components, where he encouraged audience members to brainstorm solutions to common AI-related problems.

$$\text{Inclusivity} = \frac{\text{Diverse Perspectives}}{\text{AI Development}} \qquad (49)$$

This equation became a running joke in his talks, where he would quip, "If we don't include everyone, we might as well be programming our AIs to be just as clueless as a cat trying to understand calculus!"

Impact and Reception

Rowan's ability to engage with his audience led to a surge in interest in AI education. After one particularly inspiring TED Talk, he received an influx of messages from students expressing their newfound interest in machine learning. He often joked, "If I had a dollar for every student who decided to pursue AI after one of my talks, I could fund my own AI startup!"

The reception of his talks was overwhelmingly positive, with many attendees noting that they left feeling informed and inspired. Rowan's blend of humor, relatable anecdotes, and solid theoretical grounding made him a sought-after speaker in the tech community.

Conclusion

In conclusion, Rowan Levi's public speaking engagements and TED Talks not only educated but also entertained. By breaking down complex theories into digestible pieces and engaging his audience with humor, he made the world of AI feel accessible to everyone. As he often said, "AI is not just for the techies; it's for everyone! And if we don't get it right, we might just end up with a robot that thinks it's a cat!"

Through his efforts, Rowan not only established himself as a thought leader but also paved the way for a future where technology is developed with empathy and inclusivity at its core.

Controversies and Backlash from Tech Communities

As Rowan Levi rose to prominence in the field of artificial intelligence, he found himself at the center of a storm of controversies and backlash from various tech communities. This section delves into the critical debates and issues that arose during his journey, highlighting the complexities of ethical considerations in AI development.

The Dilemma of Bias in AI

One of the most significant controversies surrounding Rowan's work involved the issue of bias in machine learning algorithms. Despite his best intentions, the algorithms he developed were scrutinized for potentially perpetuating existing societal biases. For instance, a facial recognition system he created was found to have a higher error rate for individuals from underrepresented racial groups.

This raised questions about the data sets used to train these models. As noted by [?], "Machine learning systems are only as good as the data they are trained on," which means that if the training data reflects historical biases, the resulting algorithms will likely do the same. Rowan faced backlash from activists who argued that AI should not reinforce systemic inequalities.

Public Speaking Engagements and Backlash

Rowan's advocacy for responsible AI development often put him in the crosshairs of tech communities resistant to change. During a high-profile TED Talk, he addressed the importance of ethical considerations in AI, emphasizing the need for transparency and accountability. His assertion that "AI should serve humanity, not the other way around" was met with mixed reactions.

While many applauded his vision, others in the audience felt that he was undermining the potential of AI to drive economic growth. Critics argued that his focus on ethics could stifle innovation and lead to unnecessary regulations. The backlash intensified on social media, with hashtags like #AIWhispererFail trending as detractors voiced their opinions.

Controversies in AI Governance

Rowan's push for a governance framework for AI drew ire from several prominent figures in the tech industry. He proposed a model that included diverse stakeholder representation, arguing that "AI should not be governed solely by those who create it." This idea was met with skepticism, as many industry leaders believed that such governance would slow down the pace of innovation.

In response to these concerns, Rowan cited the work of [?], who highlighted that "without inclusive governance, the risks of AI could outweigh its benefits." The debate over governance structures became a focal point of contention, with many arguing that the tech community should prioritize rapid development over ethical considerations.

The Role of Media in Shaping Perceptions

The media played a crucial role in shaping public perceptions of Rowan's work. Sensationalist headlines often exaggerated the potential dangers of AI, leading to a public outcry that sometimes overshadowed the nuanced discussions he sought to promote. For example, a report claiming that "AI Will Replace Humans by 2030" sparked widespread panic, prompting Rowan to clarify that while AI could automate certain tasks, it was not a panacea for all societal issues.

This disconnect between media narratives and the realities of AI technology fueled further backlash. Critics accused Rowan of being out of touch with the industry, while supporters praised his efforts to address the ethical implications of AI. This dichotomy illustrated the challenges faced by innovators like Rowan in navigating the complex landscape of public opinion.

Maintaining Integrity Amidst Public Scrutiny

Despite the controversies, Rowan remained steadfast in his commitment to ethical AI development. He frequently engaged with critics, participating in forums and debates to address their concerns directly. He emphasized that "true innovation must be grounded in responsibility," a mantra that resonated with many of his supporters.

However, the constant scrutiny took a toll on his mental health. He often reflected on the pressures of being a public figure in a field fraught with ethical dilemmas. In interviews, he shared that "being an innovator in AI is like walking a tightrope; one misstep can lead to a fall." This metaphor underscored the precarious balance he had to maintain between advancing technology and advocating for its responsible use.

In conclusion, Rowan Levi's journey was marked by significant controversies and backlash from tech communities. While his efforts to promote ethical AI development were met with resistance, they also sparked essential conversations about the future of technology and its impact on society. As the debate continues,

Rowan's work serves as a reminder of the importance of integrating ethical considerations into the rapidly evolving field of artificial intelligence.

Maintaining Integrity Amidst Public Scrutiny

In an era where technology advances at an unprecedented pace, the figure of the AI Whisperer, Rowan Levi, stands as a beacon of integrity amidst the tumultuous waves of public scrutiny. As he navigates the complexities of ethical considerations in artificial intelligence, Rowan embodies the delicate balance between innovation and responsibility. This section delves into the challenges he faces, the theoretical frameworks guiding his decisions, and the examples that highlight his commitment to maintaining integrity.

Theoretical Frameworks

Rowan's approach to integrity in AI can be understood through the lens of several ethical theories, primarily Utilitarianism, Deontological ethics, and Virtue ethics. Each of these frameworks offers a distinct perspective on moral decision-making, particularly in the context of AI's societal implications.

- **Utilitarianism** posits that the best action is the one that maximizes overall happiness. In the realm of AI, this translates to developing systems that benefit the greatest number of people. Rowan often emphasizes the importance of assessing the societal impact of his innovations, ensuring that they do not inadvertently harm vulnerable populations.
- **Deontological ethics**, on the other hand, argues that actions must adhere to a set of rules or duties. For Rowan, this means upholding principles of transparency, accountability, and fairness in AI development. He frequently invokes the idea that ethical guidelines should not be compromised for the sake of progress.
- **Virtue ethics** focuses on the character of the moral agent rather than the consequences of actions. Rowan strives to cultivate virtues such as honesty, courage, and empathy within the tech community. He believes that fostering a culture of integrity is essential for the sustainable development of AI.

Challenges Faced

Despite his commitment to ethical principles, Rowan faces significant challenges in maintaining integrity. The rapid pace of technological advancement often leads to a culture of "move fast and break things," where the consequences of AI applications are overlooked in the pursuit of innovation. This mindset poses ethical dilemmas, particularly when it comes to issues such as data privacy, bias in algorithms, and the potential for job displacement.

One notable example occurred when Rowan's team developed a facial recognition algorithm that demonstrated remarkable accuracy. However, upon further examination, they discovered that the model performed poorly on individuals from underrepresented backgrounds. Faced with the dilemma of releasing a flawed product that could perpetuate discrimination, Rowan opted for transparency. He publicly acknowledged the limitations of the technology and delayed its launch until further refinements were made, prioritizing ethical considerations over market pressures.

Public Engagement and Advocacy

Rowan's commitment to integrity extends beyond his personal practices; he actively engages with the public to foster a dialogue about the ethical implications of AI. Through speaking engagements, social media platforms, and community outreach programs, he addresses concerns related to AI's impact on employment, privacy, and human rights.

In his TED Talk titled "The Ethics of AI: A Call to Action," Rowan outlines the importance of including diverse voices in AI development. He argues that ethical AI cannot be achieved without understanding the perspectives of those who are most affected by these technologies. By advocating for inclusivity, he demonstrates that maintaining integrity involves not only adhering to ethical principles but also amplifying the voices of marginalized communities.

Navigating Controversies

Rowan's journey has not been without controversy. His outspoken views on responsible AI development have drawn criticism from some sectors of the tech community, particularly those focused on profit maximization. In one instance, a prominent tech CEO publicly challenged Rowan's stance on regulating AI technologies, framing it as a hindrance to innovation.

In response, Rowan maintained his composure and reiterated his commitment to ethical practices. He emphasized that the long-term success of AI depends on public trust, which can only be achieved through transparency and accountability. This incident exemplifies the challenges of maintaining integrity in a landscape where financial incentives often clash with ethical considerations.

Conclusion

In conclusion, Rowan Levi's journey as the AI Whisperer highlights the importance of maintaining integrity amidst public scrutiny. By grounding his approach in ethical theories, confronting challenges head-on, engaging with the public, and navigating controversies with grace, he sets a standard for future innovators in the field of artificial intelligence. As technology continues to evolve, Rowan's commitment to ethical principles serves as a reminder that integrity is not merely an option but a necessity for sustainable progress in AI.

Through his actions and advocacy, Rowan Levi not only advances the field of machine learning but also champions a future where technology serves humanity responsibly and equitably. In a world where the stakes are high, his legacy will undoubtedly inspire future generations to prioritize ethics alongside innovation.

Legacy and Future Prospects

Philanthropy and Giving Back

Establishing the Levi Foundation for AI Education

In a world increasingly dominated by artificial intelligence, Rowan Levi recognized a pressing need to bridge the educational gap that exists in the field of AI. Thus, he established the Levi Foundation for AI Education, a non-profit organization dedicated to empowering the next generation of innovators through access to quality education in artificial intelligence and machine learning.

Mission and Vision

The mission of the Levi Foundation is simple yet profound: to democratize access to AI education, ensuring that individuals from all backgrounds have the opportunity to learn, innovate, and contribute to the rapidly evolving tech landscape. The vision is to create a future where AI is developed responsibly and inclusively, reflecting diverse perspectives and ideas.

Addressing Educational Inequities

One of the core problems the Levi Foundation aims to tackle is the disparity in access to technology education, particularly in underrepresented communities. According to a report by the National Center for Women & Information Technology, women and minorities are significantly underrepresented in tech fields, which perpetuates a cycle of inequity. The Levi Foundation's initiatives focus on providing resources, mentorship, and scholarships to those who have historically been marginalized in the tech industry.

$$\text{Equity} = \frac{\text{Access to Resources}}{\text{Educational Opportunities}} \qquad (50)$$

This equation illustrates that true equity in education is achieved when access to resources is proportional to the availability of educational opportunities. The Levi Foundation seeks to increase both variables, ensuring that every aspiring AI professional can thrive.

Programs and Initiatives

The Levi Foundation launched several key programs to fulfill its mission:

- **Scholarship Programs:** Providing financial assistance to students pursuing degrees in AI-related fields, particularly those from low-income backgrounds.

- **Workshops and Bootcamps:** Hosting hands-on workshops and intensive bootcamps that cover topics such as machine learning, data science, and ethical AI development. These programs are designed to be accessible and engaging, often featuring guest speakers from the industry.

- **Mentorship Networks:** Connecting students with industry professionals who can provide guidance, support, and networking opportunities. This initiative aims to create a supportive community for aspiring AI innovators.

- **Online Learning Resources:** Developing a comprehensive online platform that offers free courses, tutorials, and educational materials on AI concepts, programming languages, and practical applications.

Collaborations and Partnerships

To amplify its impact, the Levi Foundation collaborates with universities, tech companies, and other non-profit organizations. These partnerships help to expand the reach of its programs and ensure that the curriculum is aligned with industry standards. For example, the foundation has partnered with local universities to create a dual-enrollment program that allows high school students to earn college credits while learning about AI.

Measuring Success

To evaluate the effectiveness of its initiatives, the Levi Foundation employs a variety of metrics, including:

- **Enrollment Rates:** Tracking the number of students participating in programs and scholarships.

- **Graduation Rates:** Monitoring the success of scholarship recipients in completing their degrees in AI-related fields.
- **Job Placement:** Assessing the employment outcomes of program participants to determine the impact on their career trajectories.

Real-World Impact

The Levi Foundation has already begun to see tangible results. For instance, in its first year, the foundation awarded over $500,000 in scholarships, resulting in a 20% increase in enrollment among underrepresented students in AI programs at partner universities. Additionally, feedback from participants indicates a high level of satisfaction with the mentorship and resources provided, with many reporting increased confidence in their abilities to pursue careers in AI.

Conclusion

The establishment of the Levi Foundation for AI Education marks a significant step toward addressing the educational inequities in the tech industry. By providing access to resources, mentorship, and financial support, Rowan Levi is not only fostering the next generation of AI innovators but also ensuring that the future of technology is inclusive and representative of diverse voices. As the foundation continues to grow, it remains committed to its mission of empowering individuals to harness the power of AI for the greater good, paving the way for a more equitable and innovative future.

Funding Scholarships and Research Grants

Rowan Levi's commitment to education and innovation is exemplified through his establishment of various scholarships and research grants aimed at nurturing the next generation of AI leaders. Recognizing the barriers that many aspiring technologists face, especially those from underrepresented communities, Rowan's initiatives are designed to provide both financial support and mentorship opportunities.

The Importance of Scholarships in Technology

In the realm of technology and artificial intelligence, access to education can be a significant hurdle. Scholarships serve as a vital mechanism for leveling the playing field, allowing talented individuals to pursue their studies without the burden of overwhelming debt. A report by the National Center for Education Statistics (NCES) indicates that students from low-income backgrounds are less likely to enroll in and complete higher education programs. By funding scholarships, Rowan aims to reduce these disparities, ensuring that financial barriers do not stifle potential innovation.

Types of Scholarships Offered

Rowan's scholarships are diverse, targeting various demographics and fields of study within AI. The scholarships include:

- **Undergraduate Scholarships:** These are aimed at high school graduates who demonstrate exceptional aptitude in mathematics and computer science. Recipients are selected based on academic performance and potential for innovation.

- **Graduate Research Grants:** Designed for graduate students conducting groundbreaking research in machine learning and artificial intelligence, these grants provide funding for projects that have the potential to contribute significantly to the field.

- **Diversity Scholarships:** Specifically targeting students from underrepresented communities in tech, these scholarships aim to promote inclusivity in the AI sector. They are awarded based on both merit and financial need.

- **Internship and Fellowship Programs:** These programs provide students with hands-on experience in leading tech companies, bridging the gap between academic learning and practical application.

Impact of Research Grants

In addition to scholarships, Rowan's foundation allocates substantial funds for research grants. These grants are critical in supporting innovative projects that may not receive funding from traditional sources. Research grants are typically awarded based on the following criteria:

1. **Innovation Potential:** Projects that introduce novel concepts or methodologies in AI are prioritized. For instance, a grant might support a project exploring unsupervised learning techniques that could lead to more efficient data processing.

2. **Feasibility:** Proposals must demonstrate a clear plan for execution, including timelines and resource allocation.

3. **Societal Impact:** Projects that address pressing global challenges—such as climate change, healthcare accessibility, or educational disparities—are particularly favored. For example, a grant could fund research on AI applications in predictive healthcare analytics.

Examples of Funded Projects

Several notable projects have emerged from Rowan's funding initiatives. One such project, led by a graduate student from an underrepresented background, focused on developing an AI algorithm for early detection of diabetic retinopathy. The project not only showcased innovative machine learning techniques but also had the potential for significant societal impact by improving healthcare outcomes for millions.

Another example is a collaborative research initiative between Rowan's foundation and a leading university, aimed at creating a comprehensive dataset for training AI models in natural language processing (NLP). This initiative was pivotal in advancing the field, as it provided researchers with the necessary resources to develop more accurate and context-aware language models.

Measuring Success

The success of Rowan's scholarship and grant programs is measured through various metrics, including:

- **Graduation Rates:** Tracking the percentage of scholarship recipients who complete their degrees.

- **Research Publications:** Monitoring the number of published papers and patents resulting from funded research projects.

- **Career Advancement:** Assessing the career trajectories of scholarship recipients, including job placements in leading tech companies and startups.

Conclusion

Rowan Levi's commitment to funding scholarships and research grants reflects his belief that education and opportunity should be accessible to all, regardless of background. By investing in the future of AI through these initiatives, he not only fosters innovation but also creates a more inclusive and diverse technological landscape. As the field of artificial intelligence continues to evolve, the impact of these scholarships and grants will undoubtedly resonate for generations to come, nurturing the next wave of innovators who will shape our world.

Supporting Underrepresented Communities in Tech

Rowan Levi's commitment to supporting underrepresented communities in technology stems from a deep understanding of the systemic barriers that many individuals face in accessing education and career opportunities in the tech industry. This section explores his initiatives, the challenges faced by these communities, and the theoretical frameworks that underpin his approach.

Understanding the Challenges

The tech industry has long been criticized for its lack of diversity. According to a report by the National Center for Women & Information Technology (NCWIT), women hold only 26% of computing jobs, and underrepresented minorities make up just 10% of the tech workforce. These statistics highlight a significant disparity that has persisted over the years.

Barriers to entry include:

- **Access to Education:** Many underrepresented communities lack access to quality education in STEM (Science, Technology, Engineering, Mathematics) fields. Schools in low-income areas often have limited resources, leading to a lack of exposure to technology and coding.

- **Financial Constraints:** The high cost of higher education can deter individuals from pursuing degrees in tech. Scholarships and funding opportunities are often not well-publicized or accessible.

- **Cultural Bias:** There exists a pervasive bias in hiring practices that favors candidates from prestigious backgrounds or institutions, often overlooking talented individuals from diverse communities.

Rowan's Initiatives

To address these challenges, Rowan established the Levi Foundation for AI Education, which focuses on creating pathways for underrepresented individuals to enter and thrive in the tech industry. His initiatives include:

- **Scholarships:** The foundation offers scholarships specifically for students from underrepresented backgrounds pursuing degrees in computer science and AI. This financial support alleviates the burden of tuition costs and encourages more individuals to enter the field.

- **Mentorship Programs:** Recognizing the importance of guidance, the foundation pairs students with industry professionals. These mentorship relationships provide invaluable insights into navigating the tech landscape, resume building, and interview preparation.

- **Workshops and Outreach:** The Levi Foundation organizes workshops in underserved communities, introducing students to coding, machine learning, and AI through hands-on projects. This practical experience demystifies technology and ignites interest in STEM careers.

- **Partnerships with Schools:** Collaborating with local schools, the foundation implements after-school programs that focus on technology and innovation. These programs aim to inspire young minds and provide them with the skills needed for future careers in tech.

Theoretical Frameworks

Rowan's initiatives are grounded in several key theories that emphasize the importance of diversity and inclusion in tech:

- **Social Capital Theory:** This theory posits that individuals gain advantages through their social networks. By facilitating mentorship and networking opportunities, Rowan helps underrepresented individuals build the social capital necessary to succeed in the tech industry.

- **Critical Race Theory (CRT):** CRT examines the ways in which race and racism intersect with other forms of social stratification. Rowan's advocacy for equitable access to technology education aligns with CRT's emphasis on addressing systemic inequalities.

- **Intersectionality:** Recognizing that individuals experience multiple, overlapping identities, Rowan's initiatives take into account the unique challenges faced by women, LGBTQ+ individuals, and people of color in tech. This holistic approach ensures that programs are tailored to meet diverse needs.

Impact and Future Directions

The impact of Rowan's efforts is already visible. Many scholarship recipients have gone on to secure internships and jobs at leading tech companies, contributing to a more diverse workforce. The mentorship programs have not only empowered individuals but have also created a ripple effect, as mentees become mentors themselves, fostering a culture of support and community.

Looking ahead, Rowan aims to expand the foundation's reach by:

- **Increasing Funding:** Securing additional funding from tech companies and philanthropic organizations to broaden scholarship offerings and program availability.

- **Advocating for Policy Change:** Engaging with policymakers to promote legislation that supports equitable access to tech education and resources.

- **Creating Online Resources:** Developing an online platform that provides free coding resources, tutorials, and community forums for underrepresented individuals interested in tech.

In conclusion, Rowan Levi's commitment to supporting underrepresented communities in tech is not just a philanthropic endeavor; it is a critical step towards building a more inclusive and innovative future. By addressing systemic barriers and providing tangible support, he is paving the way for a new generation of tech leaders who will bring diverse perspectives and solutions to the industry.

$$D = \frac{N_u}{N_t} \tag{51}$$

Where:

- D is the diversity ratio in tech,

- N_u is the number of underrepresented individuals in tech,

- N_t is the total number of individuals in tech.

Increasing N_u through initiatives like those of the Levi Foundation is essential for improving the diversity ratio D and fostering innovation in the tech industry.

AI Outreach Programs and Workshops

Rowan Levi, the self-proclaimed AI Whisperer, understood that the future of technology didn't just reside in the silicon chips and neural networks he created; it lived in the minds of the next generation. This epiphany struck him like a rogue algorithm during a particularly boring conference call, where he realized that if he didn't step in, future innovators might just be learning about AI from TikTok dances instead of textbooks. Thus, the inception of his AI Outreach Programs and Workshops began, aiming to bridge the gap between complex technology and eager young minds.

The Purpose of Outreach

The primary goal of these outreach initiatives was to demystify artificial intelligence. Rowan believed that AI should not be the exclusive domain of tech-savvy geniuses holed up in dark basements, but rather a playground for curious minds from all walks of life. He often quipped, "If I can teach my grandma how to use voice recognition software, then I can teach anyone!"

To achieve this, Rowan's workshops were designed to be engaging, interactive, and—most importantly—fun. They included hands-on activities like building simple neural networks using LEGO bricks, which, let's be honest, is the only way to truly understand the complexities of deep learning. Because if you can't explain it with LEGO, then what's the point?

Workshop Structure

Each workshop followed a carefully crafted structure:

- **Introduction to AI:** A light-hearted discussion on what AI is, sprinkled with Rowan's signature humor. He often started with, "So, who here has talked to their toaster? No? Just me?"

- **Interactive Activities:** Participants would engage in group activities, such as creating their own chatbots using simple programming tools. This hands-on experience was crucial for understanding the underlying principles of machine learning.

- **Real-World Applications:** Discussions on how AI is used in everyday life, from Netflix recommendations to self-driving cars. Rowan would emphasize, "If AI can help me find the best rom-com to binge-watch, imagine what it can do for you!"

- **Ethical Considerations:** A segment dedicated to the importance of ethics in AI. Rowan would say, "Just because we can create a robot that does the cha-cha doesn't mean we should. Let's keep the dancing to us humans!"

Challenges Faced

Despite the enthusiastic reception of these workshops, Rowan faced numerous challenges. One major hurdle was the pervasive misconception that AI was too complicated for the average person. To counter this, he crafted relatable analogies, such as comparing neural networks to the way humans learn from mistakes—"Like when you touch a hot stove and never do it again, but with data!"

Another challenge was securing funding and resources for these outreach programs. Many potential sponsors were skeptical, thinking, "Why invest in teaching kids about AI when they can just play video games?" Rowan, armed with statistics and a side of charm, often countered with, "Because today's gamers are tomorrow's innovators! Plus, if we don't teach them, who will create the next generation of AI to make video games even better?"

Success Stories

The success of these outreach programs was evident in the stories that emerged from them. One standout was a young girl named Mia, who, after participating in Rowan's workshop, developed an AI program that helped her local animal shelter match pets with potential adopters based on personality traits. "Mia's program is like Tinder for cats and dogs!" Rowan exclaimed during a local news interview, emphasizing the impact of teaching practical AI applications.

Another success story involved a group of high school students who, inspired by Rowan's workshops, went on to win a national competition with their AI project aimed at reducing food waste in their community. Rowan proudly stated, "They took the 'waste' out of waste management—now that's innovation!"

Conclusion

Rowan Levi's AI Outreach Programs and Workshops were not just about teaching the next generation how to code; they were about inspiring a movement. By equipping young minds with the knowledge and tools to harness the power of AI responsibly, Rowan was not only shaping the future of technology but also ensuring that it was a future where everyone could participate.

As he often said, "AI isn't just for the tech elite; it's for anyone who's ever wondered how to make their life easier—like automating the dishes. Now that's a future I want to be part of!" And with that spirit, Rowan continued to push boundaries, one workshop at a time, proving that the best innovations often come from the most unexpected places—like a community center filled with kids and a whole lot of enthusiasm.

Leaving a Lasting Impact on the Field

Rowan Levi's journey through the landscape of artificial intelligence (AI) has not only been marked by personal achievements but also by a profound commitment to leaving a lasting impact on the field. His understanding of the ethical implications of AI, combined with his innovative research, has positioned him as a pivotal figure in shaping the future of technology.

At the core of Rowan's legacy is his establishment of the Levi Foundation for AI Education, which aims to democratize access to AI knowledge and resources. The foundation focuses on three primary areas: funding scholarships for underrepresented students, providing research grants for innovative projects, and facilitating outreach programs that introduce AI concepts to younger generations. This initiative is crucial in addressing the gender and racial disparities prevalent in the tech industry. According to a report by the National Center for Women & Information Technology (NCWIT), women and minorities are significantly underrepresented in computing fields, with women holding only 26% of computing jobs and Black and Hispanic individuals making up only 11% and 8% respectively. By targeting these disparities, Rowan aims to cultivate a new wave of diverse talent in AI.

One of the foundation's flagship programs is the "AI for Everyone" workshop series, which travels to schools in underserved communities. These workshops not only teach basic programming skills but also introduce students to the ethical dimensions of AI. For example, during a session, students learn about the algorithmic bias that can occur in machine learning models. They explore how biases in training data can lead to unfair outcomes, such as facial recognition systems misidentifying individuals from certain racial backgrounds. This hands-on approach empowers students to think critically about the technology they will one day help to create.

Rowan's commitment to ethical AI development is further exemplified in his research, particularly in the area of responsible machine learning. He has published several influential papers addressing the need for transparency in AI algorithms. In his seminal work, "Understanding the Black Box: A Framework for Transparent AI," he proposes a model that incorporates explainability into machine learning systems. The equation governing this model can be expressed as:

Transparency = f(Model Complexity, Feature Importance, User Understanding)

where f is a function that quantifies how different factors contribute to the overall transparency of an AI model. By advocating for this framework, Rowan encourages developers to build systems that not only perform well but can also be understood by their users, thereby fostering trust and accountability in AI technologies.

Moreover, Rowan's influence extends to his active participation in public discourse surrounding AI ethics. His TED Talks, which have garnered millions of views, tackle pressing issues such as the implications of AI on employment and human rights. In one particularly memorable talk, he humorously juxtaposes the rise of AI with the fears of a robot takeover, stating, "If a robot ever tries to take my job, it better come with a sense of humor and a good Yelp review!" This blend of humor and serious commentary resonates with audiences, making complex topics accessible and engaging.

Rowan also spearheaded initiatives that encourage collaboration between tech companies and academic institutions. By fostering partnerships that prioritize ethical research, he has played a crucial role in creating a more responsible AI ecosystem. For instance, he helped launch the "AI Ethics Consortium," which brings together industry leaders, researchers, and policymakers to discuss the social implications of AI technologies. This consortium has produced guidelines that emphasize the importance of ethical considerations in AI development, such as ensuring data privacy and promoting fairness in algorithmic decision-making.

In conclusion, Rowan Levi's legacy is characterized by his unwavering commitment to fostering diversity, promoting ethical practices, and encouraging collaboration in the field of AI. Through his foundation, research, public speaking, and community outreach, he is not only shaping the future of technology but also ensuring that it is inclusive and responsible. As he often states, "The future of AI isn't just about smarter machines; it's about smarter people making smarter choices." This philosophy encapsulates his vision for a world where technology serves humanity, rather than the other way around.

Speculations and Predictions for AI's Future

What Lies Ahead for Machine Learning?

As we peer into the crystal ball of machine learning, we find ourselves at the cusp of a revolution that promises to redefine the boundaries of technology and human interaction. The future of machine learning (ML) is not just about algorithms and data; it's a complex tapestry woven with the threads of ethics, creativity, and unprecedented capabilities. Here, we explore the trajectories that machine learning might take, the challenges that lie ahead, and the theoretical advancements that could steer its course.

Theoretical Advancements

One of the most exciting prospects for the future of machine learning is the development of more sophisticated algorithms that can learn from fewer examples. Current models, particularly deep learning networks, require vast amounts of labeled data to perform well. This dependency raises questions about data availability and the ethical implications of data collection practices. Theoretical advancements such as **few-shot learning** and **transfer learning** aim to mitigate these issues.

$$L_{few-shot} = \sum_{i=1}^{n} \mathcal{L}(f(x_i), y_i) + \lambda \cdot \mathcal{R}(f) \tag{52}$$

where $L_{few-shot}$ is the loss function for few-shot learning, f is the model function, x_i are the input examples, y_i are the corresponding labels, and $\mathcal{R}(f)$ is a regularization term to prevent overfitting, with λ as the regularization parameter.

As we develop models that require less data, we also need to address the issue of **explainability**. As machine learning systems become more integrated into critical decision-making processes, the demand for transparency will grow. Future research will likely focus on creating algorithms that not only perform well but also provide understandable justifications for their predictions.

Challenges Ahead

Despite the promise of machine learning, several challenges loom on the horizon. One significant issue is the **bias in algorithms**. Machine learning models are only as good as the data they are trained on, and if that data reflects societal biases, the models will perpetuate and even exacerbate these biases. Addressing this challenge requires a multi-faceted approach, including:

1. **Diverse Data Collection**: Ensuring data is representative of all demographics. 2. **Bias Detection Tools**: Developing algorithms that can identify and mitigate biases in training datasets. 3. **Ethical Guidelines**: Establishing industry-wide standards for ethical AI development.

Real-World Applications

Looking ahead, the applications of machine learning will expand dramatically across various sectors. In healthcare, for instance, machine learning algorithms will play a pivotal role in predictive analytics, enabling early detection of diseases. The incorporation of **reinforcement learning** in treatment planning could lead to personalized medicine, where algorithms adapt to individual patient responses.

In the realm of environmental science, machine learning can help tackle climate change by optimizing energy consumption and predicting environmental changes. For example, models that analyze satellite imagery can provide insights into deforestation patterns and urban sprawl, aiding in conservation efforts.

$$E_{opt} = \min \sum_{t=1}^{T} C(t) \cdot P(t) \qquad (53)$$

where E_{opt} is the optimized energy consumption, $C(t)$ is the cost of energy at time t, and $P(t)$ is the predicted energy usage at that time.

Machine-Human Collaboration

The future of machine learning will also see a shift toward **collaborative intelligence**, where humans and machines work together to enhance decision-making processes. This collaboration will require the development of systems that can understand human nuances, emotions, and contexts. For instance, customer service bots will evolve from simple query handlers to empathetic companions capable of understanding customer sentiment and responding appropriately.

Conclusion

In conclusion, the future of machine learning is a blend of opportunity and responsibility. As we advance towards a world where machines can learn and adapt, it becomes crucial to prioritize ethical considerations and strive for inclusivity in data representation. The potential for machine learning to solve complex global challenges is immense, but it is imperative that we navigate this journey with caution and foresight. The trajectory of machine learning will ultimately depend on our ability to harness its power responsibly, ensuring that it serves as a tool for positive change in society.

As Rowan Levi often says, "If we can teach machines to learn, we can certainly teach ourselves to think critically about how we use them."

AI's Role in Solving Global Challenges

Artificial Intelligence (AI) is not just a futuristic concept reserved for science fiction; it is a powerful tool that has the potential to address some of the most pressing global challenges we face today. From climate change to healthcare, AI's capabilities can be harnessed to create innovative solutions that improve lives and sustain our planet. In this section, we will explore how AI can play a pivotal role in tackling these challenges, supported by theories, practical applications, and real-world examples.

Climate Change and Environmental Sustainability

Climate change is arguably the most significant challenge of our time. Rising temperatures, extreme weather events, and biodiversity loss threaten our ecosystems and livelihoods. AI can contribute to climate action in several ways:

- **Predictive Modeling:** AI algorithms can analyze vast datasets to predict climate patterns and model the potential impacts of climate change. For instance, machine learning models have been developed to forecast sea-level rise and its implications for coastal cities.

- **Energy Efficiency:** AI can optimize energy consumption in buildings and industries. Smart grids powered by AI can predict energy demand and adjust supply accordingly, reducing waste. A notable example is Google's DeepMind, which has successfully reduced energy usage in data centers by up to 40% through machine learning algorithms that optimize cooling systems.

- **Sustainable Agriculture:** AI technologies, such as precision farming, utilize data from sensors and satellites to enhance crop yields while minimizing environmental impact. For instance, IBM's Watson Decision Platform for Agriculture integrates AI with IoT and blockchain to help farmers make informed decisions about planting, watering, and harvesting.

The integration of AI in these areas not only mitigates climate change but also fosters a sustainable future.

Healthcare and Disease Management

The healthcare sector is another domain where AI can make a substantial impact. With the global population aging and the prevalence of chronic diseases on the rise,

AI technologies can revolutionize how we approach healthcare delivery and disease management:

- **Disease Diagnosis:** AI-driven diagnostic tools can analyze medical images and patient data with remarkable accuracy. For example, Google's DeepMind developed an AI system that can detect over 50 eye diseases as accurately as expert ophthalmologists, enabling earlier intervention and treatment.

- **Drug Discovery:** The process of drug discovery is notoriously time-consuming and expensive. AI algorithms can analyze chemical compounds and predict their interactions, significantly accelerating the discovery of new medications. Atomwise, a startup using AI for drug discovery, has partnered with research institutions to identify potential treatments for diseases like Ebola and multiple sclerosis.

- **Personalized Medicine:** AI can analyze genetic information and patient histories to tailor treatments to individual needs. This approach not only improves patient outcomes but also reduces the likelihood of adverse effects. Companies like Tempus leverage AI to analyze clinical and molecular data, facilitating personalized treatment plans for cancer patients.

By improving diagnosis, treatment, and drug development, AI can enhance healthcare systems and save countless lives.

Poverty Alleviation and Economic Development

AI can also play a crucial role in addressing poverty and promoting economic development, particularly in low-income regions:

- **Financial Inclusion:** AI-driven fintech solutions can provide access to financial services for underserved populations. Mobile banking applications using AI algorithms can assess credit risk and offer microloans to individuals who lack traditional banking access. For instance, M-Pesa in Kenya has transformed the financial landscape by enabling mobile payments and savings for millions.

- **Job Creation and Skill Development:** While there are concerns about AI displacing jobs, it also has the potential to create new employment opportunities. AI can identify skill gaps in the labor market and facilitate training programs that equip individuals with the necessary skills for future jobs. Platforms like Coursera leverage AI to recommend personalized learning paths based on users' backgrounds and career goals.

- **Smart Urban Planning:** AI can assist in designing and managing urban environments, making cities more livable and sustainable. By analyzing data on traffic patterns, public transportation, and resource allocation, AI can inform urban planning decisions that improve infrastructure and reduce inequality.

Through these applications, AI can contribute to economic growth and poverty reduction, fostering a more equitable society.

Ethical Considerations and Challenges

While the potential of AI to solve global challenges is immense, it is essential to address the ethical considerations and challenges that accompany its deployment:

- **Bias and Fairness:** AI systems can perpetuate biases present in training data, leading to unfair outcomes. Ensuring that AI models are trained on diverse datasets and regularly audited for bias is crucial to achieving equitable solutions.

- **Data Privacy:** The use of personal data in AI applications raises concerns about privacy and consent. Transparent data practices and robust regulations are necessary to protect individuals' rights while harnessing the power of AI.

- **Accountability:** As AI systems become more autonomous, determining accountability for their decisions becomes increasingly complex. Establishing clear guidelines for accountability and responsibility in AI deployment is essential to maintain public trust.

Addressing these ethical challenges is vital to ensuring that AI serves humanity positively and responsibly.

Conclusion

In conclusion, AI holds significant promise in addressing global challenges such as climate change, healthcare, and poverty alleviation. By leveraging its capabilities, we can create innovative solutions that improve lives and foster a sustainable future. However, it is imperative to navigate the ethical considerations associated with AI to ensure that its deployment is responsible and equitable. As we move forward, the collaboration between technologists, policymakers, and communities will be crucial in harnessing AI for the greater good, paving the way for a brighter tomorrow.

Ethical Considerations for AI Governance

The rapid advancement of artificial intelligence (AI) technologies has raised significant ethical considerations that must be addressed to ensure responsible governance. As AI systems become increasingly integrated into various aspects of society, the implications of their use necessitate a framework that prioritizes ethical standards, accountability, and transparency.

The Need for Ethical Frameworks

AI governance involves the establishment of guidelines and regulations that dictate how AI technologies should be developed and utilized. These frameworks are essential to mitigate risks associated with AI systems, such as bias, privacy violations, and unintended consequences. The **Ethics Guidelines for Trustworthy AI** published by the European Commission outlines key principles for AI governance, including:

- **Human Agency and Oversight:** Ensuring that AI systems support human decision-making and do not undermine human autonomy.

- **Technical Robustness and Safety:** Developing AI systems that are resilient, secure, and operate within defined safety parameters.

- **Privacy and Data Governance:** Safeguarding personal data and ensuring transparency in data usage.

- **Transparency:** Providing clear and understandable information about AI systems and their decision-making processes.

- **Diversity, Non-Discrimination, and Fairness:** Promoting inclusivity and preventing bias in AI algorithms and applications.

Challenges in AI Governance

Despite the establishment of ethical frameworks, several challenges persist in the governance of AI:

1. **Bias and Discrimination:** AI systems can perpetuate existing biases present in training data. For instance, a study by [?] demonstrated that facial recognition systems exhibited higher error rates for women and people of color due to biased datasets. This raises concerns about fairness and equality in AI applications.

2. **Accountability:** Determining accountability for AI decisions can be complex. When an autonomous vehicle is involved in an accident, questions arise regarding liability—should the manufacturer, software developer, or the vehicle owner be held responsible? This ambiguity complicates legal frameworks and societal trust in AI technologies.

3. **Privacy Concerns:** The collection and processing of vast amounts of personal data by AI systems pose significant privacy risks. The **General Data Protection Regulation (GDPR)** in the European Union aims to protect personal data, but enforcement remains a challenge, particularly in cross-border scenarios.

4. **Rapid Technological Advancement:** The pace at which AI technology evolves can outstrip the development of regulatory frameworks. Policymakers often struggle to keep up with innovations, leading to gaps in governance that can be exploited.

Case Studies in AI Governance

To illustrate the ethical considerations in AI governance, several case studies highlight both successful implementations and failures:

Case Study 1: The COMPAS Algorithm The Correctional Offender Management Profiling for Alternative Sanctions (COMPAS) algorithm is used in the United States to assess the risk of re-offending among criminal defendants. A ProPublica investigation revealed that the algorithm disproportionately flagged Black defendants as higher risk compared to white defendants, raising serious ethical concerns about bias in predictive policing tools [?].

Case Study 2: AI in Hiring Several companies have adopted AI-driven recruitment tools to streamline the hiring process. However, a notable instance involved Amazon scrapping an AI recruitment tool that favored male candidates over female candidates, as the algorithm learned from historical hiring patterns that were biased against women. This case underscores the importance of ensuring fairness and transparency in AI systems used for employment decisions [?].

The Role of Stakeholders in AI Governance

Effective AI governance requires collaboration among various stakeholders, including:

- **Governments:** Establishing regulatory frameworks and standards for AI development and deployment.

- **Industry Leaders:** Implementing ethical practices within organizations and promoting transparency in AI systems.

- **Academics and Researchers:** Conducting studies on the societal impacts of AI and providing evidence-based recommendations for governance.

- **Civil Society:** Advocating for ethical AI practices and holding organizations accountable for their AI systems.

Conclusion

In conclusion, the ethical considerations for AI governance are multifaceted and require a proactive approach to ensure that AI technologies serve the public good. By prioritizing ethical frameworks, addressing challenges, and fostering collaboration among stakeholders, society can harness the potential of AI while mitigating its risks. As Rowan Levi continues to advocate for responsible AI development, his work will be pivotal in shaping the future landscape of AI governance, ensuring that innovation does not come at the expense of ethical integrity.

Speculations on Machine-Human Collaboration

The future of machine-human collaboration is poised to redefine the boundaries of innovation, creativity, and productivity. As we stand on the brink of an era where artificial intelligence (AI) can augment human capabilities, it is essential to explore the potential synergies that can arise from this collaboration. This section delves into the theoretical frameworks, challenges, and real-world examples that illustrate the transformative power of machine-human partnerships.

Theoretical Frameworks

The concept of machine-human collaboration can be anchored in several theoretical frameworks. One prominent theory is the **Distributed Cognition Theory**, which posits that cognitive processes are not confined to an individual but are distributed across people, tools, and environments. This theory suggests that machines can serve as cognitive partners, enhancing human decision-making and problem-solving abilities.

Mathematically, we can represent the collaborative process as follows:

$$C = H + M \qquad (54)$$

where C represents the collaborative output, H is the human input, and M is the machine input. This equation highlights that the synergy between human and machine can yield results that neither could achieve independently.

Another relevant framework is the **Human-Centered AI** approach, which emphasizes the importance of designing AI systems that prioritize human needs and values. This approach advocates for transparency, interpretability, and user empowerment, ensuring that machines enhance human capabilities rather than replace them.

Challenges in Collaboration

Despite the promising prospects, several challenges must be addressed to facilitate effective machine-human collaboration. One significant issue is the **Trust Gap**. Humans often exhibit skepticism towards AI systems, particularly when it comes to critical decision-making processes. To bridge this gap, it is essential to develop AI systems that can explain their reasoning and provide justifications for their recommendations.

For example, in the context of healthcare, AI algorithms can assist doctors in diagnosing diseases. However, if a physician is presented with a diagnosis generated by an AI system without a clear explanation, they may hesitate to trust the machine's judgment. This highlights the need for explainable AI (XAI) frameworks that can articulate the rationale behind machine-generated conclusions.

Examples of Successful Collaboration

Several real-world examples demonstrate the potential of machine-human collaboration across various domains. In the field of **creative arts**, AI tools like OpenAI's DALL-E and ChatGPT have enabled artists and writers to explore new creative avenues. For instance, a writer might use an AI language model to generate plot ideas, which they can then refine and expand upon, resulting in a richer narrative. This collaborative dynamic showcases how machines can serve as creative partners, sparking inspiration and innovation.

In the realm of **manufacturing**, companies like Siemens have implemented AI-driven predictive maintenance systems that work alongside human operators. These systems analyze data from machinery to predict failures before they occur, allowing human workers to intervene proactively. This collaboration not only enhances operational efficiency but also ensures the safety of human workers by reducing the risk of equipment malfunctions.

Future Directions

Looking ahead, the evolution of machine-human collaboration will likely be influenced by advancements in several key areas. One area of focus is the development of **affective computing**, which aims to create machines that can recognize and respond to human emotions. By understanding emotional cues, AI systems can tailor their interactions to better support human users, fostering a more intuitive collaborative experience.

Furthermore, as AI systems become more integrated into daily life, the concept of **collective intelligence** will gain prominence. This approach leverages the strengths of both humans and machines to solve complex problems. For instance, crowdsourcing platforms can harness the collective wisdom of diverse human contributors, while AI algorithms can analyze and synthesize the gathered insights, leading to more informed decision-making.

In conclusion, the future of machine-human collaboration holds immense promise, but it also requires careful consideration of ethical implications and societal impacts. As innovators like Rowan Levi advocate for responsible AI development, it is crucial to ensure that these collaborations enhance human capabilities while prioritizing transparency, trust, and inclusivity. By addressing the challenges and embracing the opportunities presented by machine-human partnerships, we can pave the way for a future where technology and humanity work hand in hand to tackle the world's most pressing challenges.

Rowan Levi's Personal Goals and Aspirations

Rowan Levi, known as the AI Whisperer, has always been more than just a brilliant mind in machine learning; he is a visionary with aspirations that reach beyond his impressive academic and professional achievements. As he stands at the forefront of AI innovation, his personal goals reflect a deep understanding of the ethical implications and societal responsibilities that accompany technological advancements.

Empowering the Next Generation

One of Rowan's primary aspirations is to inspire and empower the next generation of innovators in AI and technology. He believes that education is the cornerstone of progress, and he is committed to making AI knowledge accessible to all, particularly underrepresented communities. To achieve this, he has launched initiatives that include:

- **Workshops and Seminars**: Conducting hands-on workshops in schools and community centers, where students can learn about AI through engaging, practical projects. For example, he developed a workshop titled "AI for Everyone," where participants build their own simple neural networks using user-friendly software.

- **Mentorship Programs**: Establishing mentorship programs that connect aspiring technologists with experienced professionals in the field. Rowan often emphasizes the importance of guidance, stating, "A single conversation can spark a lifetime of curiosity."

Advocating for Ethical AI Development

Rowan recognizes that with great power comes great responsibility. As AI continues to permeate various aspects of life, he is determined to advocate for ethical AI development. His goals in this area include:

- **Creating Ethical Frameworks**: Collaborating with policymakers and technologists to establish ethical guidelines for AI usage. He often cites the need for transparency, accountability, and fairness in algorithms, as encapsulated in the equation:

$$\text{Ethical AI} = \frac{\text{Transparency} + \text{Accountability} + \text{Fairness}}{\text{Bias} + \text{Misuse}}$$

This equation highlights that ethical AI can only thrive when transparency, accountability, and fairness are prioritized over bias and misuse.

- **Public Discourse**: Engaging in public discussions and debates about the implications of AI technology on society. He frequently participates in panels where he addresses concerns about job displacement due to automation, arguing that while AI can replace certain tasks, it also creates opportunities for new roles that require human creativity and emotional intelligence.

Innovating for Global Challenges

Rowan's aspirations extend to using AI as a tool for solving some of the world's most pressing challenges. He envisions a future where technology is harnessed to address issues such as climate change, healthcare disparities, and poverty. His specific goals include:

- **AI for Climate Action**: Developing machine learning models that predict environmental changes and optimize resource management. For instance, he is currently working on a project that utilizes AI to analyze satellite imagery for deforestation tracking, aiming to provide actionable insights for conservation efforts.

- **Healthcare Innovations**: Pioneering AI applications that improve healthcare outcomes, particularly in underserved areas. Rowan is passionate about using predictive analytics to enhance disease prevention strategies, as expressed in his statement: "If we can predict, we can prevent."

Personal Growth and Lifelong Learning

Beyond his professional aspirations, Rowan is committed to personal growth and lifelong learning. He believes that to remain relevant in an ever-evolving field, one must continuously seek knowledge and new experiences. His personal goals in this realm include:

- **Pursuing Diverse Interests**: Engaging in activities outside of AI, such as art and philosophy, to foster creativity and critical thinking. He often shares that reading literature has helped him approach problem-solving from unique perspectives.

- **Balancing Work and Life**: Striving to maintain a healthy work-life balance, Rowan emphasizes the importance of mental health in sustaining creativity and innovation. He practices mindfulness and encourages others to take breaks, stating, "Sometimes, the best ideas come when you're not trying to find them."

Conclusion

Rowan Levi's personal goals and aspirations reflect a holistic vision for the future of AI—one that intertwines innovation with ethical responsibility, social impact, and personal growth. As he continues to navigate the complexities of the AI landscape, his commitment to empowering others and advocating for responsible technology ensures that his legacy will extend far beyond his individual achievements. In the words of Rowan, "The future of AI is not just about machines; it's about the people who use them."

Index

a, 4, 5, 7–11, 13–17, 19–26, 29–31, 33–40, 43–45, 47, 49–51, 53–58, 60–66, 68–75, 77–79, 82, 84, 85, 87, 88, 90–94, 96, 98–100
ability, 13, 24, 26, 30, 36, 40, 49, 50, 54, 62, 90
academia, 33, 42, 49, 61
academic, 4, 9, 10, 13, 16, 25, 38, 39, 47, 50, 54, 88, 98
acceptance, 29, 31
access, 66, 77–79
accomplishment, 16
accountability, 68, 71, 74, 99
accuracy, 19, 23, 54, 61, 74
act, 39
action, 19, 91
activation, 33
activity, 35
Adam, 18
adaptability, 57
adaptation, 57
addition, 39, 61
address, 26, 50, 56, 72, 82, 93, 100
adoption, 45
adrenaline, 4
adult, 7
advancement, 73

advocacy, 64, 68, 71, 75
advocate, 13, 26, 96, 98, 99
age, 25
aging, 91
AI, 64
aim, 22
Alan Turing, 13
alarm, 4
algebra, 14
algorithm, 23, 25, 43, 45, 56, 61, 74
alleviation, 93
allure, 25
ambition, 25
amount, 21
Angela Chen, 25
application, 30, 35, 45, 57
appreciation, 55
approach, 13, 39, 44, 45, 55–57, 61, 64, 66, 69, 73, 75, 82, 87, 92, 96
architecture, 16, 17, 19, 32, 33
area, 87, 99
aroma, 38
art, 62
ascent, 60
aspect, 55
assembly, 4, 65
assertion, 71

attempt, 8
attendee, 54
attention, 24, 26, 32, 33, 37
attitude, 7
audience, 50
audits, 68
autonomy, 57
availability, 78
award, 61

backlash, 71, 72
backpropagation, 18
balance, 39, 40, 72, 73
batch, 19
beacon, 73
beginning, 5
behavior, 13, 35, 57
being, 13, 38, 72
belief, 26, 31
Bellman, 21
benefit, 39
bias, 18, 35, 56, 65–67, 71, 74, 87, 99
biodiversity, 91
birthday, 7, 10, 39
blend, 10, 34, 50, 64, 88, 90
blur, 9
brain, 16
brainstorming, 16
branch, 26
break, 74
breakthrough, 10, 34
breeding, 4
brilliance, 60
building, 4, 9, 40, 55, 57, 84
bulb, 4

calculator, 10, 55
call, 29

capital, 29
car, 4
carbon, 59
career, 5, 16, 22, 25, 26, 38, 39, 50, 53, 55, 62, 82
case, 66, 95
cat, 20, 31, 37
catapult, 4
caution, 90
center, 71
chain, 58
chair, 31
challenge, 34, 36, 38, 61, 91
change, 7, 16, 22, 24, 26, 71, 90, 91, 93, 100
changer, 54
chatbot, 38
Chen, 25
cherry, 26, 30
child, 5, 7, 69
childhood, 5, 15, 16
class, 10
classroom, 36
climate, 22, 24, 26, 90, 91, 93, 100
club, 4
code, 25
coding, 16, 25
coffee, 38
collaboration, 22, 35, 36, 50, 56, 57, 61, 62, 88, 94, 96, 98
collaborator, 61
collection, 65
college, 78
color, 69
combat, 67
combination, 13, 23, 26, 64
commentary, 50, 88
commitment, 22, 24, 36, 38, 51, 53, 55, 56, 64, 66, 68, 72–75,

Index 105

79, 82, 84, 87
committee, 30
communication, 51
community, 4, 21, 22, 31, 43, 51, 55, 56, 60, 74, 84
company, 36, 54
competition, 53
complexity, 21
component, 30
composure, 74
compromise, 39
computer, 10, 34, 40
concept, 13, 26
conclusion, 24, 34, 38, 42, 66, 72, 75, 84, 90, 93, 96, 98
conference, 21, 35
confetti, 10
confidence, 4
confusion, 7
consciousness, 13
consent, 55, 57
conservation, 90
consideration, 23, 61, 67, 98
consortium, 88
consumption, 60, 90
context, 37, 73
controversy, 74
convolution, 43
core, 16, 40, 49, 55, 70
cornerstone, 4, 43, 57, 99
course, 8
Covey, 38
creativity, 3, 9, 10, 13
credibility, 54
criticism, 21, 74
cross, 18
crowd, 10
culmination, 16, 29, 31
culture, 62, 69, 74, 84

curiosity, 5, 7, 9, 16, 19, 29, 45
curriculum, 78
curve, 21
cutting, 36

dance, 38
data, 10, 11, 16, 22, 23, 25, 26, 35, 43, 45, 55, 57, 58, 61, 65–67, 69, 74, 87, 88, 90
dataset, 19
day, 16, 87
deadline, 30
debate, 72
debugging, 16
decision, 23, 25, 26, 33, 38, 57, 61, 73, 88
dedication, 24, 29, 31
deforestation, 90
delivery, 68, 92
demand, 58
deployment, 65, 68, 93
depth, 13, 50
descent, 19
design, 55, 57
desire, 25, 26
determination, 7, 19, 29
development, 13, 22, 24, 25, 35, 38, 45, 47, 53, 56, 63–66, 68, 71, 72, 74, 87, 88, 92, 96, 98, 99
diagnosis, 92
dialogue, 64, 74
dichotomy, 72
dignity, 68
dilemma, 39, 74
disaster, 8
disconnect, 72
discourse, 88
discrimination, 56, 66, 74

discussion, 62
disease, 92
disguise, 8
displacement, 74
display, 24
dive, 8, 34
diversity, 62, 83
domain, 85, 91
downtime, 58
drug, 92

ease, 30
economy, 66
ecosystem, 88
edge, 36, 56
education, 77–79, 82, 99
effect, 84
effectiveness, 54, 78
efficiency, 54, 55, 58, 64, 66
effort, 7
Emily Tran, 20
empathy, 70
emphasis, 57
employment, 65, 66, 74, 88
encouragement, 7
end, 38, 55
endeavor, 7, 36, 68, 84
energy, 59, 60, 90
enforcement, 56
engagement, 38, 57, 64
engineer, 7
enrollment, 78
entropy, 18
entry, 82
environment, 4, 5, 7, 36, 38, 39
epoch, 19
equation, 4, 15, 21, 23, 32, 48, 53, 61, 65, 67, 78, 87, 99
equipment, 58

equity, 78
era, 73
error, 26, 71
establishment, 79, 94
ethnicity, 56
evaluation, 66
event, 10, 26
examination, 74
example, 13, 37, 54, 56, 57, 66, 72, 74, 78, 87, 90
excellence, 10
exclusion, 67
exercise, 25
expense, 65, 96
experience, 16, 24, 35, 38, 40, 55, 62
experiment, 5, 8, 10
expert, 61
expertise, 51, 60, 62, 64
explainability, 87
exploration, 34
exposure, 5

face, 10, 65, 79, 82
faculty, 35
failure, 4, 5, 7–9, 26
fair, 4, 10, 16, 26
fairness, 56, 67, 68, 88, 99
fall, 72
fascination, 4, 5, 15, 16, 25
father, 4
feature, 23
feedback, 21, 38, 57
fervor, 5, 34
fiction, 13
field, 5, 13, 19, 22, 24, 25, 27, 34–36, 42, 45, 47, 50, 51, 53, 56, 57, 60, 62, 64, 69, 71–73, 75, 77, 100
figment, 13

Index

figure, 21, 53, 64, 72, 73
finance, 47, 57
finesse, 38
fire, 16
flagship, 87
flexibility, 66
focus, 37, 55
footprint, 59
force, 68
forecast, 22, 60
forefront, 53, 65, 99
foresight, 90
formation, 35
foster, 50, 62, 74, 93
foundation, 5, 15, 24, 34, 40, 78, 79, 84, 87
framework, 5, 13, 58, 61, 65, 71
friend, 39
function, 18, 19, 32
future, 5, 7, 9–11, 13, 16, 24, 30, 34, 38, 42, 45, 47, 50, 55, 57, 60, 62–64, 68, 70, 72, 75, 77, 79, 84, 90, 91, 93, 96, 98, 100

gadget, 30
game, 54
gap, 42, 49, 65, 77
garage, 4
garden, 5
gender, 56
generation, 69, 77, 79, 84, 99
gift, 7
gig, 36, 66
glare, 31
glitch, 8
goal, 85
good, 24, 68, 79, 88, 94, 96
governance, 71, 72, 94–96

grace, 75
grade, 10
gradient, 19
grandma, 85
ground, 4
groundbreaking, 42, 43, 46, 50, 62
grounding, 75
groundwork, 7, 9, 13, 16, 38, 47
group, 34, 35
growth, 21, 40, 93, 100
guest, 14, 16, 39
guidance, 11, 22, 25

hackathon, 35
hallmark, 13, 57
hand, 98
hardware, 4
head, 41, 75
health, 22, 35, 72
healthcare, 47, 49, 57, 61, 66, 91–93, 100
heart, 30
hindrance, 74
hiring, 56, 66
hobby, 5
home, 4, 7
homework, 9
household, 4
human, 13, 16, 22, 26, 40, 42, 47, 55, 57, 62, 65, 66, 68, 74, 88, 98
humanity, 25, 57, 64, 71, 75, 93, 98
humor, 20, 24, 50, 68, 88
hurdle, 14, 21

idea, 13, 25, 72
image, 43, 45
imagery, 90
imagination, 13, 22

imaging, 45
impact, 22, 25, 26, 49, 51, 54, 57, 60, 62, 65, 66, 68, 72, 74, 78, 84, 91
imperative, 68, 90, 93
implementation, 66
importance, 3, 11, 13, 24, 25, 31, 35, 37, 38, 40, 62, 65, 66, 71, 73–75, 83, 88
improvement, 26
incident, 8, 39, 40, 66, 74
inclusion, 83
inclusivity, 65, 70, 74, 90, 98
income, 92
incorporation, 47
increase, 78
individual, 57, 60
industry, 33, 35, 38, 39, 49, 50, 54, 61, 63, 71, 72, 78, 79, 82, 84, 88
inefficiency, 61
inequality, 65
influence, 47, 55, 63, 88
information, 16, 21
infrastructure, 54
ingredient, 29
initiative, 35, 61
innovation, 4, 5, 16, 22, 25, 36, 53, 58, 60, 61, 64, 66, 72–75, 79, 96, 99
innovator, 7, 13, 16, 22, 24, 30, 38, 72
input, 16
installation, 62
instance, 35, 56, 64–66, 71, 74, 88
instruction, 4
integration, 54, 56, 91
integrity, 73–75, 96
intellect, 10

intelligence, 5, 7, 9, 13, 16, 19, 27, 36, 38, 43, 45, 47, 50, 51, 53, 58, 60, 69, 71, 73, 75, 77, 85
interaction, 21, 57
interest, 25
interface, 54
internship, 36, 38
interpretability, 61
interpretation, 43
intersection, 45, 60
introduction, 64
inventory, 58
ire, 71
issue, 26, 71

job, 53, 64, 66, 74, 88
journey, 5, 7, 9, 14, 16, 19, 22, 24, 29, 38, 40, 47, 53, 71, 72, 74, 75, 90
joy, 31

Kate Crawford, 56
key, 40, 64, 78, 83
kid, 30
kind, 5
kit, 4, 7–9
knack, 20, 30
knowledge, 7, 10, 11, 16, 22, 45, 50, 56, 99, 100

labor, 64
lack, 66
landscape, 45, 55, 57, 62, 66, 72, 74, 77, 96
language, 21, 25, 40, 42, 54
launch, 74, 88
law, 56
layer, 17
leader, 36, 51, 55, 63, 64, 70

Index

leadership, 11
learning, 5, 7, 8, 10, 11, 13–16, 18–24, 26, 32, 34–36, 38, 40, 43, 45–47, 50, 54, 55, 57, 58, 60, 61, 63, 71, 75, 77, 78, 87, 90, 98, 100
legacy, 50, 60, 75
lens, 73
lesson, 8
letter, 29, 30
leverage, 45, 61
Levi, 47
life, 4, 7, 25, 38–40, 42, 62, 69, 85, 99
lifecycle, 68
limit, 22
line, 4, 65
literature, 47
living, 7
loss, 18, 19, 32, 56, 91
love, 15
luck, 29

machine, 5, 7, 10, 11, 13–16, 19–24, 26, 32, 34–36, 38, 40, 43, 45, 47, 50, 54, 55, 57, 58, 60, 61, 63, 71, 75, 77, 87, 90, 98
machinery, 58
maintenance, 58, 60
major, 39
making, 13, 25, 33, 37, 38, 57, 61, 68, 73, 88, 99
malfunctioning, 8
management, 38, 40, 58–60, 92
manner, 24, 54
mantra, 25, 56, 72
manual, 4, 64
manufacturing, 58, 64

Marcus Chen, 61
market, 74
mat, 37
maximization, 74
maze, 11, 15, 16
measure, 18
mechanism, 32, 37
media, 24, 35, 72, 74
mentor, 25
mentorship, 19, 21, 22, 25, 26, 35, 38, 79, 84
merit, 26
metaphor, 72
method, 15
methodology, 55, 57
milestone, 16
mind, 5, 98
mindset, 74
mini, 7, 19
minority, 65
mischief, 9
mission, 77–79
misstep, 72
misuse, 55, 99
mitigation, 24
mix, 34
model, 10, 16, 18–20, 22–24, 26, 37, 48, 49, 56, 58, 61, 71, 74, 87
moment, 15, 16, 24, 31, 38
morning, 29
mother, 8

nature, 5, 11, 13
navigation, 45, 61
necessity, 75
need, 35, 66, 67, 69, 71, 77, 87
nerd, 29
network, 16, 20, 38, 43

networking, 34, 39
niche, 55
Nick Bostrom, 56
night, 16
nosedive, 8
novel, 4, 61
number, 19

obsession, 4
off, 61
on, 4, 7, 8, 10, 13, 15, 17, 21–23, 25, 26, 29, 30, 33–35, 37–39, 41, 47, 50, 53–55, 57, 58, 60–63, 65, 66, 69, 72–75, 82, 84, 87, 88, 90, 91
one, 17, 23, 26, 35, 69, 72, 74, 87, 88, 100
operation, 43, 49
opinion, 72
opportunity, 8, 50, 77, 90
optimization, 58–61
optimizer, 18
option, 75
organization, 77
other, 63, 71, 78
outcry, 72
output, 16
outreach, 51, 74, 85

pace, 72, 73
pain, 54
panacea, 72
panic, 72
paper, 35
parameter, 18
part, 7, 35
participation, 62, 88
party, 10, 39
passion, 4, 9, 11, 13, 16, 24, 26, 31

Patel, 21, 61
path, 26
patient, 57, 61
people, 5, 55, 69
performance, 18, 25, 38
period, 16
perseverance, 31, 45
personality, 30
perspective, 13, 21, 47, 55, 62, 73
phase, 23, 53
philanthropic, 84
philosophy, 4, 34
physics, 30
picture, 16
piece, 8, 16
pioneer, 5, 25
place, 4, 8, 11, 16, 24, 35
plan, 8
playground, 85
point, 25, 50, 54
policing, 56
pooling, 33
population, 91
positive, 26, 38, 90
potential, 4, 13, 24, 45, 47, 54–57, 72, 74, 90, 93, 96
poverty, 92, 93, 100
power, 19, 25, 31, 35, 43, 45, 56, 79, 90, 99
practice, 56
practitioner, 26
precursor, 5, 21
prediction, 23
preparation, 23
presentation, 24, 38
pressure, 38
prevalence, 91
principle, 55, 65
prioritization, 40

Index

privacy, 55, 56, 65, 74, 88
problem, 45, 56, 60, 61, 69
process, 14, 16, 20, 21, 53, 55, 57, 61, 66, 97
processing, 21, 25, 45, 54
product, 74
professional, 40, 68, 78, 98, 100
profile, 71
profit, 74, 77, 78
program, 78
programming, 87
progress, 62, 75, 99
project, 4, 7, 9, 10, 15, 22–26, 34, 35, 39, 54, 56, 62
prominence, 50, 58, 71
promise, 93, 98
promotion, 66
protection, 66
prowess, 47, 53, 55
psychology, 56
public, 63, 64, 72–75, 88, 96
purpose, 18, 38
pursuit, 7, 74
push, 53, 60, 71
puzzle, 16

quality, 23, 45, 77
quo, 36

radar, 53
Raj Patel, 21
rate, 18, 71
ratio, 54, 67
reach, 78, 84, 98
reality, 31
realization, 26
realm, 58, 90, 100
recognition, 24, 26, 43, 45, 65, 69, 71, 74, 85, 87

recommendation, 30, 57
recruiting, 66
reduction, 93
reenactment, 8
reflection, 16
refrain, 4
regression, 10, 20, 23
reinforcement, 15, 21, 26, 46, 47, 58, 61
relationship, 55, 65
relevance, 26, 50
reminder, 62, 73, 75
report, 72
representation, 71, 90
representative, 79
reputation, 61
research, 5, 13, 21, 33–35, 41, 42, 47, 49, 50, 54–56, 62–64, 79, 87, 88
researcher, 20, 35
resilience, 4, 9
resistance, 72
reskilling, 65
resolve, 26
respect, 18
response, 74
responsibility, 24, 25, 56, 69, 72, 73, 90, 99
result, 19
retirement, 66
review, 56, 88
rigor, 38
rise, 34, 50, 58, 88, 91
risk, 67
robot, 4, 7, 8, 11, 15, 16, 88
robotic, 64
role, 7, 19, 72, 88, 92
room, 7

Rowan, 3–5, 7–11, 13–27, 30–36, 38–42, 47, 49, 50, 53–65, 67, 68, 70–75, 79, 80, 82–85, 87, 88, 99, 100
Rowan Levi, 36, 38, 42, 44, 47, 51, 53, 55, 58, 64, 66, 69, 71, 73, 75, 77, 79, 96, 98
Rowan Levi's, 5, 7, 9, 13, 16, 19, 22, 24, 26, 29, 34, 36, 38, 40, 42, 43, 45–47, 50, 55, 57, 60, 62, 66, 68, 72, 75, 79, 82, 84
rush, 4

s, 3–5, 7–11, 13, 16, 19, 21–26, 29–32, 34–36, 38–43, 45–47, 49, 50, 55–64, 66, 68, 71–75, 79, 80, 82–84, 87, 88, 98–100
satellite, 90
schedule, 39
scholarship, 84
school, 4, 9, 10, 13, 16, 20, 25, 78
schooler, 10
science, 4, 10, 13, 16, 20, 26, 34, 40, 90
scrutiny, 72, 73, 75
sea, 24
section, 43, 55, 71, 73, 82
sector, 64, 91
security, 66
seedling, 5
self, 37
sense, 16, 38, 88
sentence, 37
series, 69, 87
session, 35, 87
set, 4, 7, 10, 26, 43, 50, 55, 58
shape, 42, 68

shoebox, 4
significance, 39, 50
skepticism, 72
skill, 4, 38
socializing, 39
society, 25, 57, 62, 68, 72, 90, 93, 96
sociology, 56
soda, 10
software, 69, 85
solar, 4
solving, 45, 100
spark, 9, 16
speaker, 14, 16, 50, 54, 63, 68
speaking, 24, 51, 63, 74
spirit, 21, 22
sprawl, 90
spring, 29
sprinkle, 9, 29
stage, 10, 24, 50
staircase, 8
stakeholder, 71
stance, 74
standard, 57, 68, 75
standout, 24
startup, 61
status, 36, 43
stem, 67
step, 79, 84
stone, 4
store, 4
storm, 71
strategy, 38
string, 4, 47
stroke, 29
structure, 23, 85
struggle, 21, 38
student, 16, 25
study, 80
style, 51

Index

subsection, 58
success, 4, 5, 7, 9, 40, 45, 74
summary, 7, 13, 50, 57, 62
summer, 36
sundae, 30
supply, 58
support, 22, 31, 79, 84
surveillance, 65
sustainability, 4
switch, 4
system, 4, 56–58, 71

table, 34
tackle, 16, 27, 30, 34, 35, 88, 90, 98
takeover, 88
talk, 88
tapestry, 9
teacher, 30
team, 11, 32, 35, 38, 56, 57, 74
teamwork, 62
tech, 14, 43, 53–55, 57, 63, 71, 72, 74, 77–79, 82–85, 88
technology, 5, 8, 9, 13, 16, 24–26, 33, 42, 45, 51, 55, 57, 60–62, 64, 65, 70, 72–75, 79, 82, 87, 98–100
TechNova, 36, 38
temperature, 24
term, 38, 74
terrain, 7
testament, 31, 45
testing, 56, 66, 67
theme, 13
theory, 56
thinker, 30
thinking, 3
thirst, 10
thought, 51, 53, 55, 62–64, 70
threat, 69

thrill, 4, 25
ticket, 36
tightrope, 72
time, 7, 10, 25, 35, 38–40, 45, 47, 57, 58, 91
toaster, 8
toll, 72
tomorrow, 64, 94
tool, 56, 57, 66, 90, 100
top, 26, 30
topic, 33
touch, 72
trade, 61
training, 11, 20, 66, 69, 87
trajectory, 7, 47, 90
Tran, 20, 22
transformation, 30
transformer, 32
transition, 69
transparency, 55, 57, 61, 65, 68, 71, 74, 87, 98, 99
treasure, 7
treatment, 92
tree, 23
trial, 26
trip, 4
troubleshooting, 4
trove, 7
trust, 57, 74, 98
tunnel, 4
turn, 4, 7, 8, 16, 53
turning, 25, 30

understanding, 5, 13, 14, 16, 19, 26, 34, 36, 38, 42, 55, 56, 62, 63, 74, 82, 99
universe, 29
university, 27, 29, 31, 34, 36, 38, 40, 47, 50

upskilling, 65
urgency, 22, 38, 65
usage, 60
use, 26, 72, 85
user, 38, 54, 55, 57
utilization, 55

validation, 67
variety, 78
vehicle, 45
versatility, 45
victory, 31
video, 8
view, 57
vision, 38, 53, 77
visionary, 98
visualization, 57
voice, 47, 85
volcano, 10

walking, 72

wave, 11
way, 16, 21, 26, 29, 45, 47, 57, 60, 69–71, 79, 84, 94, 98
weather, 91
weight, 18
well, 21, 38, 40, 45
while, 4, 24, 38, 40, 61, 66, 72, 78, 96, 98
willingness, 4
wind, 4
wisdom, 8
work, 21, 24, 31, 34, 35, 43, 45–47, 54–58, 61, 69, 71–73, 87, 96, 98
workforce, 84
workshop, 85, 87
world, 5, 9, 13, 14, 16, 19, 24–26, 35, 36, 42, 47, 50, 55, 67, 69, 75, 77, 90, 98, 100